D0763688

Pacific Hawk

John Vader

BB

DRA-314

Editor-in-Chief: Barrie Pitt
Art Director: Peter Dunbar

Military Consultant: Sir Basil Liddell Hart
Picture Editor: Robert Hunt

Executive Editor: David Mason
Designer: Sarah Kingham
Special Drawings: John Batchelor
Cartographer: Richard Natkiel
Cover: Denis Piper
Research Assistant: Yvonne Marsh

Copyright © 1970 by John Vader

First printing: July 1970
Printed in United States of America

Ballantine Books Inc.
101 Fifth Avenue New York NY 10003

Contents

Indestructible fighter

Introduction by Barrie Pitt

During the six months after the attack on Pearl Harbor, in a burst of military energy which astonished the world, Japanese military and naval forces secured dominion over half the Pacific, menaced the borders of India, completely overran the Dutch Eastern Empire and established bases from which an invasion of northern Australia seemed not only feasible, but highly probable.

As early as 19th February 1942, Port Darwin had been bombed in a devastating attack which in many ways equalled that on Pearl Harbor in ferocity and accuracy, and in the weeks and months which followed it became obvious to all in the area that the focal point of the coming struggle would be Port Moresby on the southeastern shore of New Guinea. It was upon this port that the eyes of the Japanese Admiral Yamamoto were fixed, and it was here that Allied planners decided to stand and fight whatever the cost, 'regardless of the fact' as John Vader coolly points out 'that there was no strong force of infantry, no artillery of any consequence, few anti-aircraft guns and only a small RAAF force of six Catalina flying-boats and seven Hudsons'.

This decision, made at the highest level, had far-reaching consequences, in the Battle of the Coral Sea, in the landings at Milne Bay, in the Battle of the Bismarck Sea; in the dour and courageous battles fought by Kanga Force, and finally and overwhelmingly in the battles of the Kokoda Trail. Here it was that Australian militiamen stopped the ever-spreading wave of Japanese aggression and demonstrated at last the hollowness of the myth of Japanese invincibility.

It was in these battles that the American fighter, the P-40 Hawk, played so vital a part, justifying the affection of the pilots who flew it, and displaying an amazing toughness of construction. The chief opponent of the Kittyhawk in these battles was the Zero; and the Zero was more manoeuvrable, had a higher rate of climb and a service ceiling over 3,000 feet higher. Moreover the Zero was more heavily armed and had a greater range, which often meant a greater operational time in the fighting area over New Guinea.

But the Kittyhawk was tougher and heavier, so that she could endure much more punishment and still remain in action – and in a dive she was the faster and thus potentially the more lethal weapon. Perhaps most important of

all, the men who flew the P-40s successfully had absorbed the teaching of that great American aviator Claire Chennault who laid it down 'If you take the best characteristics of your own plane and fight with them, never letting the enemy fight with the best characteristics of his plane, then you can lick him!'

How the pilots of the Kittyhawks used the advantages of their aircraft becomes clear in the following account of their exploits by John Vader, already an acknowledged expert on air-fighting as revealed in his earlier book in this series on the Spitfire.

It was not only in the South west Pacific Area that the Kittyhawks helped to hold back the advance of Axis conquest. In North Africa too, the air battles were often fought out by P-40s and an opponent just as redoubtable as the Zero – the famous Me-109. Here again, the sheer toughness and weight of the Kittyhawk often proved the decisive factor against an aircraft whose capabilities were theoretically far superior; as long, of course, as the pilots were superior. When a German ace of the near-genius of Hans-Joachim Marseille arrived on the scene, his

ability to exploit the best characteristics of the Me-109 to the full spelt disaster for Allied pilots.

But it was in the Pacific that the Kittyhawks fought the majority of their battles – from Port Darwin in the south to the Aleutians and Alaska in the north, and Myitkyina in the west. The Japanese were the enemy to be beaten, the Zero the chief antagonist, and in the end, as the book demonstrates, the Kittyhawk, in all her variations and modifications, emerged the winner. Although the last of over 14,000 P-40s had come off the assembly lines in December 1944, Kittyhawks were still operational in Borneo against isolated pockets of Japanese resistance when the war ended.

It was a remarkable achievement for an aircraft which never caught the popular imagination by its 'thoroughbred lines' or spectacular success, and which was constantly denigrated by armchair aviators on grounds of apparent statistical inferiorities.

Only the men who flew her knew the inherent virtues of the Kittyhawk; she had to be fatally wounded before harm could come to her pilot.

The tough P-40

The American P-40, like the British Hurricane, was one of the most useful aircraft to be in service at the beginning of the war and to survive, in modified form, until the end: both fighters became all-purpose workhorses after they had served first in a purely interceptor role, filling the emergency gap before faster and more versatile machines were produced to counter the superior fighter aircraft developed by the enemy; both contributed to Allied victories in the air against German, Italian and Japanese fighters; and both were transformed into bomb carriers, 'Hurri-bombers' and 'Kitty-bombers', to attack targets on land and sea when low-level bombing was the only sure way of hitting the enemy. Fighter-bombers became a vital tactical arm of the ground forces.

Neither aircraft received the same glamorous publicity accorded the Spitfire, yet without the Hurricane and P-40 the war could well have been lost—at the Battle of Britain, in North Africa's Western Desert, or in the defence of Port Moresby, the final major objective in the Japanese plan to control South East Asia.

This is a history of P-40 Hawk aircraft and particularly of the vital actions fought at Darwin, Port Moresby and Milne Bay during those months in 1942 when a few fighters and bombers, supporting a small Allied army, halted Japanese expansion and consolidation in the South West Pacific. These months were the most anxious period of the war, when Axis forces were victoriously entrenched throughout much of Europe and Asia, when Japanese warships marauded virtually unchallenged across the Pacific and Indian oceans, and when hordes of enemy troops were preparing to isolate Australia, the potential naval, military, aircraft and supply base for Allied defence and retaliation. Had Port Moresby fallen, New Guinea, the last island bastion to the north of Australia, would have been lost and the Japanese High Command could well have been tempted to invade at least the continent's port and airfield areas in Queensland, Northern Territory and Western Australia. Because it was the only fighter available in any quantity, the P-40 was sent up to cope with an enemy confident from many past victories with his superlative Zero fighter.

When the Japanese navy aircraft attacked Pearl Harbor, the first of them downed in combat in the Pacific war fell to the guns of a P-40B Tomahawk; in all, a few radial-engined P-36A Hawks and P-40B Tomahawks shot down seven Japanese planes. The Americans flew from the emergency landing field at Haleiwa where the 47th Pursuit Squadron had moved for gunnery practice. One P-40 pilot, Lieutenant George Welsh, almost achieved the score of an ace, shooting down four of the enemy. The first Japanese aircraft shot down over the Philippines was also the victim of a P-40B, flown by Lieutenant Randall B Keator of the 20th Pursuit Squadron.

Pre-war American interceptor pursuit planes were not designed to fight at heights above 20,000 feet; the P-40 performed at its best below 15,000 feet, a handicap overcome by adopting suitable tactics, learned the costly, hard way in action against high-performance enemy planes. The demand of the US Army airmen of the 1930s was for low-altitude fighters suitable for ground attack and coastal defence operations, with the accent on ruggedness of construction, and by the time the P-40 first went into action it was a thoroughly tested, tough machine, although somewhat obsolete compared with the Mitsubishi A6M Zero or Messerschmitt Bf 109. Serving with the Flying Tigers in China and the RAF and RAAF in the Western Desert in 1941, P-40 Tomahawks proved they could take heavy punishment from enemy fire and rough airfield conditions.

Sturdy on its large, wide-apart wheels, its deep body providing a cockpit of armchair proportions, its wings forming a stable gun platform and capable of lifting heavy weights of fuel, guns, ammunition and bombs, the P-40 trundled across the airfields and airstrips of many theatres of war.

'The P-40 is the strongest ship in the world. It's heavy as hell, but that makes it out-dive just about anything, and it'll out-dive the Japs two to one,' an American Volunteer Group pilot informed Robert L Scott,

who wrote of his AVG experiences in *God is My Co-Pilot*. He described what happened to a Warhawk – P-40E – that had mixed it with eight or nine Zeros: big holes in the tail, wings and fuselage, the instrument panel shot away, rudder pedals partly shot to pieces. Not only was the armour plate of the pilot's seat badly bent, but explosive bullets had driven out the rivets, shooting them into the pilot's back; he escaped the Zeros in a power dive and made a safe wheels-up belly landing.

This security of toughness could not always be relied upon to protect the pilot but it saved the life of RAAF Squadron Leader Howie Brydon later in the war when 82 Squadron was based on a dusty Pacific strip. Brydon had run into a cloud of dust on take-off and, climbing too quickly to avoid it, had stalled; the P-40N Kittyhawk flicked over and down onto the ground where it rolled over several times and was smashed to pieces. Although badly shaken, Brydon was fit enough to walk away from the wreckage.

The P-40 could not turn with a Zero and whenever they met for the first time Allied pilots resisted, if they could, taking the Japanese on in a dogfight. General Claire Chennault, head of the AVG, advised his pilots never to turn with the more manoeuvrable Zero: 'If you take the best characteristics of your plane and fight with it, never letting the enemy fight with the best characteristic of his plane, then you can lick him!' This man led his fighters to more victories than defeats against the enemy in hundreds of clashes, some of them fighter to fighter, head-on with tracer and collision avoided at the last moment.

Ten weeks after Pearl Harbor, Japanese aircraft, land-based and carrier-borne, were winging their way across the Timor Sea to effect the second most damaging attack on an Allied naval base; the objective was Port Darwin on the coast of Australia's Northern Territory.

A second Pearl Harbor

Using captured territories and isolated islands in the Pacific as stepping stones in an encircling and consolidating movement, the Japanese were ready within a few weeks of Pearl Harbor to seal off the Pacific west of the International Date Line, along the islands north of Australia and up to Indo-China. As early as January 1942 fresh Japanese troops bypassed the major South East Asian battle areas to land on islands thousands of miles from their homeland, on New Ireland, New Britain (to establish an important base at Rabaul) and on Flores and Sumba Islands. Thus they were east and west of New Guinea, controlling the South West Pacific Area and threatening the South Pacific Area at a critical time when the Allies were short of trained and experienced troops, having lost their main forces of American, British, Dutch and Australian armies captured or cut off in Malaya, the Philippines and the Netherlands East Indies; their naval forces were minimal compared with the mighty Japanese Combined Fleet and the Japanese air forces were completely superior in ship-borne and land-based fighters and bombers.

Rabaul was a serious loss for it provided the enemy with a good harbour and two airstrips. The invasion force, accompanied by two aircraft-carriers and several cruisers and destroyers, had only a small garrison to overcome. Royal Australian Air Force strength was one bomber – a Hudson stripped to act as a fighter – and eight two-seater Wirraways, the Australian-built NA-33 trainer and general purpose aircraft. Two Wirraways on patrol attacked the main pre-invasion bomber and fighter force, but the hopelessly outclassed and outnumbered Australians were quickly shot down, one Wirraway crash-landing with both crewmen wounded. The other aircraft of 24 Squadron took off as the warning came through, one Wirraway crashing on take-off, the five remaining climbing slowly but hopefully to intercept; the unscathed enemy fighters shot down three more, one crash-landing with its wounded pilot, after his observer, who had been thrown out in the spin, had parachuted to safety. Two Wirraways survived, though one had part of its tail-plane shot away, after a hide-and-seek with Zeros in and around the bright cumulus clouds. When Squadron Leader Lerew appealed to headquarters for fighters he was signalled the reply, usually expected in those days: 'Regret inability to supply fighters. If we had them you would get them.'

Silhouette of conquest; Aichi 99 'Val' dive bomber attacks

Thus, on 2nd January, the encirclement of New Guinea had begun and Japanese plans were prepared for the capture of Port Moresby, situated on the drier, southern side of the Papuan arm of eastern New Guinea and separated from Australia by a couple of hundred miles, across the Coral Sea. Timor, the Dutch and Portuguese controlled island 400 miles northeast of Darwin, was the nethermost part of the NEI chain and the next Japanese objective after the capture of Flores and Sumba Islands. Java was still Allied territory where Dutch, British and American troops were reinforced by Australians returning from the Middle East, their air forces supplied with additional aircraft ferried through Darwin and Timor. The island's main aerodrome at Penfui had been extended and improved by RAAF engineers, and there was a satellite airfield and an emergency landing strip. If Java were to survive, Timor would be a useful transit base but it was soon to become more useful to the Japanese. They captured the island after landing the 228th Regiment and paratroops of the 3rd Yokosuka Special Naval Landing Force at Dili, Kupang and on the main aerodrome on 20th February. The small force of Australians on Timor took to the hills where they successfully conducted guerilla operations for many months.

An attempt had been made to reinforce Timor despite the reluctance of General Wavell, commander of the American, British, Dutch and Australian forces (ABDA), to risk the loss of more troops in isolated areas before the overwhelming Japanese advance. The US cruiser *Houston*, destroyer *Peary* and the RAN sloops *Swan* and *Warrego* escorted four transports carrying the Australian Imperial Forces' 2/4th Pioneer Battalion, a troop of anti-tank guns and a battalion of the US 148th Field Artillery Regiment. The convoy was shadowed by a Japanese flying-boat and the captain of the *Houston* requested fighter cover. At Darwin,

the closest base, there were just two fighters – P-40s. One of these USAAF planes flew off from the RAAF station to intercept. It did not return and was never heard of again. The second Kittyhawk was sent out but the pilot failed to find the enemy or the convoy, which was duly bombed the following day, the 16th. There were some near-misses and ABDA Command ordered the convoy back to Darwin.

P-40s and P-39s were the most numerous types of fighters in the USAAC when the Pacific war started on 7th December. Altogether they numbered about 1,600 and were spread from the Aleutians to Java. The RAF and RAAF had been supplied with P-40Es which they named Kittyhawks. The USAAF named the same type Warhawks, but in the Pacific theatre they were universally referred to as Kittyhawks. The garrison on Timor had watched these and other US fighters and dive-bombers pass through Penfui aerodrome, refuelling on their way to the futile defence of Java. Few of the pilots had the training necessary to embark on long ferry flights, let alone go into action. In *Suez to Singapore* Cecil Brown describes a landing on an outback field in Northern Territory:

'A few minutes later twelve P-40Es, the Kittyhawks, came in. This is a huge field at Daly Waters – in many respects a perfect field. There are no barriers and visibility is excellent on all sides. We stood beside our bombers, watching the Kittyhawks circle to follow the leader down. The leader made a perfect landing, the next one bounced but got down. The next one seemed to be coming down too low, short of the aerodrome, and heading for a field. He came down in the field and hit a ditch. The next one did the same – down on the field and half turned over. The following Kittyhawk did the same. Lieutenant Rose was shouting and screaming, "What the

Wirraway; one of the Allied planes slaughtered by Japanese fighters

12

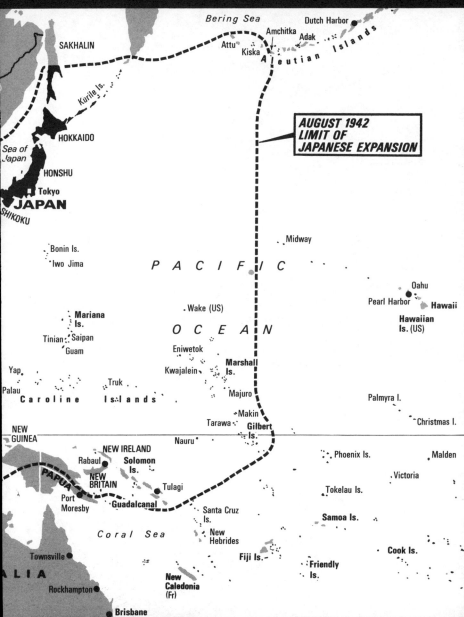

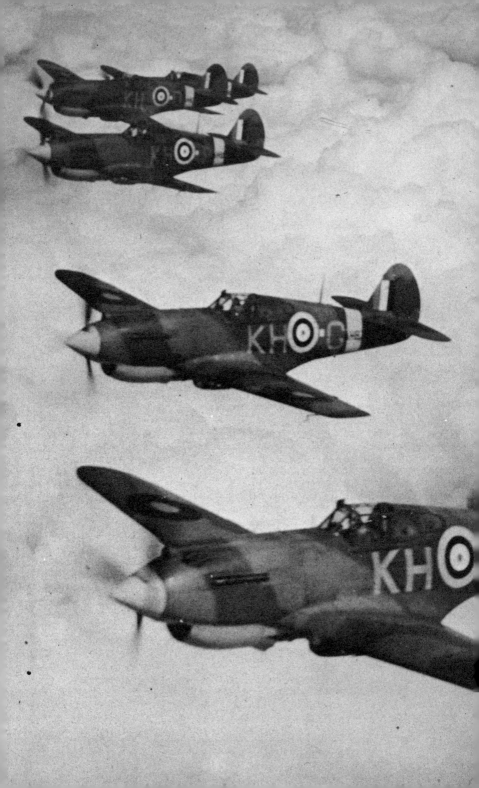

hell's the matter with them? They've got all the field in the world here to land on and they are coming down in the grass and weeds."

'The others came in all right, until the final one of the twelve. He made five attempts to get down but when four or five feet off the ground he decided he couldn't make it, put on the gas, and zoomed up and away again for another circle. Five times he did that.

"You can just imagine", Lieutenant Rose said, "what that poor kid in there is going through."

'A sergeant mechanic with us said, "The only way we'll get him down is to shoot him down."

'I remarked to some of the airmen standing by that if a pilot couldn't make a simple landing in a strange and good field, how could he fight in combat, when the enemy is on his tail?

"These boys are going to be slaughtered out here," one pilot said.

'He finally came down on the aerodrome, and unlike the three others, did not crack up. These pilots were youngsters just out of flying school, with insufficient experience. There's no help for that, I suppose. Men, even untrained, are needed desperately if Java is to be saved.'

Sometimes even moderately experienced pilots found it awkward to make decent landings on strange fields after a long flight.

Inexperience caused further losses of P-40s. A flight of nine Kittyhawks from 3 Pursuit Squadron became lost near Timor when their Liberator bomber escort, navigating for them, could not find the field and returned: eight pilots bailed out and one was killed attempting a crash-landing in the jungle. During the last few days of Timor's existence as an Allied base, two Hudson bombers, all that were left of a flight, did duty as fighter cover for patrolling Catalinas, flew

Tomahawk IIs of 403 Squadron in formation

high and low bombing missions, and watched the movement of enemy shipping through the island-dotted seas. In these last few days the two bombers flew two missions daily, up to six hours each flight, until the Japanese landed.

There had been a slow trickle of bombers, mostly Flying Fortresses and Hudsons, and Catalina flying boats, across the newly opened South Pacific ferry route. Fighter aircraft had to be brought in by sea transport. US Air Force command had been established at Melbourne, then the centre of Australian military and political control. Despite the desperate confusion and dire need for equipment in the Allies' island bases at the beginning of the conflict there were, surprisingly, dismantled P-40s unloading at Brisbane by the end of December. These were taken to assembly hangars at Amberley and Archerfield, RAAF stations near Brisbane, where fitters worked three shifts a day so that assembly continued through the twenty-four hours nonstop. By 14th January there were seventeen P-40s ready to fly and seventeen pilots – thirteen from the Philippines and four from Hamilton Field, California – forming 17 Pursuit Squadron (Provisional) – which flew off on the long journey to Java and Sumatra.

The *President Polk* arrived with an additional fifty-five P-40Es, enough to form three more provisional pursuit squadrons – the 3rd, 20th and 33rd. Some of these aircraft were also flown to Java while others were recalled from the flight and were assigned to the forming of 8, 35 and 49 Pursuit Groups. Normally a US squadron was equipped with eighteen aircraft, when they were available. By the end of 1942 the number rose to twenty-five and, in the high production year of 1945, to forty-two fighters. Three pursuit squadrons formed a pursuit group, titles which were officially changed to fighter squadrons and fighter groups in May

17

1942. The 1930s image of the brightly painted, 'streamlined' biplane fighters, screaming as the wind rushed through their struts in 200mph attacks, was gone; the colourful 'pursuit ships' had been replaced by drab green and brown monoplane 'fighters'.

Australia's service arms were severely depleted by January 1942. Three experienced divisions of the AIF were in the Middle East, two of them prepared to return as soon as shipping became available, and a fourth division was trapped in Malaya. Many of the RAN warships were with RN flotillas and 6,500 RAAF-trained aircrew were serving in RAF and RAAF squadrons in Europe, the Middle East and South East Asia. In the RAAF at this time there were less than fifty modern operational aircraft – bombers and flying-boats but no fighters. And the eighty Wirraway trainers were being rapidly depleted.

When the commander at RAAF Darwin sent off first one then the other American Kittyhawks to hunt the Japanese flying-boat over the Timor convoy, he was unaware that ABDA Command had ordered fifteen Kittyhawks, being flown from Brisbane to Perth, to divert to Darwin *en route* to Java and to give protection to the convoy on the way. From Perth the seaplane tender *Langley* and the transport *Seawitch* were to have carried these with another fifty-nine P-40s, some as deck cargo and some crated, to Java. When she arrived there, the *Langley* was sunk by enemy aircraft on 27th February and the crated planes which had been unloaded were destroyed when the Japanese landed two days later. Of the fifteen Kittyhawks diverted to Darwin, five were lost in accidents on the way up and the rest, under Major Floyd 'Slugger' Pell, arrived at the RAAF

Immediate radial-engined precursors of the P-40. *Above :* P-36A of the 20th Pursuit Group. *Below :* P-36C of 27th Pursuit Squadron

station. So, on Darwin's fatal day, 19th February, there were at the RAAF station Pell's ten fighters plus the lone P-40 piloted by Lieutenant J G Oestreicher, a remnant of the 3rd Pursuit gone on to Java or crashed over Timor. The total air strength in the RAAF's North Western Area also included seventeen Hudson bombers (eight without crews), seventeen Wirraways (five unserviceable), a Liberator bomber in transit, a Fairey Battle, three de Havilland Moth Minors, two Beechcraft transports and another Beechcraft at Bathurst Island.

It was obvious that Darwin would be attacked by enemy bombers; the few warships, merchantmen, the port's facilities, the hangars and airfields were choice targets for the Japanese who were about to invade Timor. Anything military at Darwin was a potential threat to these operations. Allied Intelligence could predict a slow build-up of the enemy's land-based attack aircraft but there was no means of tracking the greater danger – Admiral Nagumo's carrier force. Darwin was isolated from the more populated areas of Australia, connected to the south by an uncompleted narrow-gauge railway and dirt roads. The higher commands considered Java to be a more worthwhile area to build up and Admiral King, Chief of the US Naval Staff at the time, said that 'Darwin, not entirely suitable from the beginning, was becoming untenable.' Except for able-bodied men, most of the civilian population had been evacuated in January. If the strong defences of Malaya and the Philippines could not prevent invasion there seemed little hope that the small garrison of artillery and Militia (the called-up Australian civilian military force, equivalent to the US National Guard, all other Australian forces being volunteers) could throw back a Japanese attack in force, nor could the few small warships and almost non-existent air force.

Major Pell's squadron of ten had been given orders to continue on to Java despite all the indications that Darwin would shortly be attacked. Shipping had been bombed and an enemy submarine had been sunk near the port; on 28th January an unidentified aircraft flew to within a couple of miles of the town; on 30th January the Qantas flying-boat *Corio* was shot down near Kupang; there was an air raid alert on 8th February and Japanese aircraft were sighted over Timor; a single-engined monoplane, unidentified, circled Darwin on the 10th, and, on the 16th and 18th, there were further reconnaissances by single aircraft, obviously 'Photo Joe' covering the port and airfields. Despite this well-known prelude to a bombing attack, the P-40s were to continue that morning on their flight to Java. Fortunately for the gesture of defiance and the surprise their presence was to offer the Japanese, the dawn take-off was delayed because of mechanical trouble, and after they got away at 0915hrs bad weather ahead caused Major Pell to bring his planes back.

While that flight was taking place, approaching from the sea was another, flown by the Japanese navy's most able aircrews from Admiral Nagumo's task force of aircraft-carriers *Akagi*, *Kaga*, *Soryu* and *Hiryu*, escorted by fourteen cruisers and destroyers, also supported by Admiral Kondo's two battleships, three heavy cruisers and several destroyers. This raid was to be Nagumo's biggest since his attack on Pearl Harbor.

As had happened on numerous other occasions, the first warnings of imminent attack were ignored. A priest on Melville Island reported by radio to Darwin that a large formation of aircraft coming from the north west had passed and that his mission had been strafed by an enemy fighter.

Flying boats which played their part in the Pacific. *Above:* Qantas 'C' Class *Below:* Catalina

A while later an artillery officer reported seeing a Kittyhawk dive into the sea, and airmen at the RAAF Darwin station thought they could observe overhead was the American fighters in training. The Kittyhawks were in action before the air-raid sirens sounded, and the army were asking one observer how he decided that the aircraft he saw were Japanese ('They've got bloody great red spots on them' was the reply) when the bombs began to fall.

Major Pell had followed the rules after returning from the sortie towards Timor, leaving one flight in the air while the other landed to refuel. None of his pilots was experienced except Oestreicher, who led the cover patrol of five P-40s at 15,000 feet, while Pell took his flight of five down to the roadside strip called Hughes. The eleventh P-40 had not taken off because of unserviceability. Oestreicher was still climbing to his patrol height when a Zero attacked from above; he called out 'Zero!' and turned to face the enemy.

'On their first attack they broke our formation and forced us to dive out, dropping our belly tanks as we went,' Oestreicher reported. The scattered P-40s did not include Lieutenant Wieks, number four man in the flight; his radio was dead and he had not heard the warning. 'I thought Peres had engine trouble and was heading back to the airfield,' reported Wieks. 'I tried to catch up with Oestreicher and Perry to fill the gap left by Peres. Suddenly below me and to my right I saw that Peres was being followed by another plane. Then I saw the red circle insignia and was galvanised by the realisation that here was my very first Japanese Zero. I remembered turning on my gunsight and switching my gas tanks, while all the time watching the pursuit below me and trying to turn in such a way as to get in behind the Zero chasing Peres. As I turned I saw the Jap fire his cannon. I saw shells hitting Peres, and then his plane slowly rolled over

and down.' (Reported in Douglas Lockwood's *Australia's Pearl Harbor*.)

Perry was shot down into the harbour and Lieutenant Walker, the fifth member of the flight, wounded and with his plane shot up, landed intact and managed to get to a slit trench before Japanese cannon fire destroyed his P-40. Wiek's plane was hit and while it was in a flat spin he bailed out into the bay's shark-infested water, floating in his Mae

West and swimming for some time before the the fast flood tide carried him, during the evening, back to land. Oestreicher took advantage of cloud cover while he chose his first victims, two Val dive-bombers at 15,000 feet; one he sent down flaming, and he saw smoke belch from strikes on the other. His were the first aerial victories over Australian soil.

Major Pell and the other four pilots had no time to get into action before they were attacked. One pilot was killed on the ground while Pell and the three others who managed to get their Kittyhawks airborne were almost immediately attacked. Pell's plane was hit and he bailed out at eighty feet, but his parachute barely opened and he was badly injured from the fast drop. Then he was killed on

Early type Flying Fortresses on the field at Port Moresby

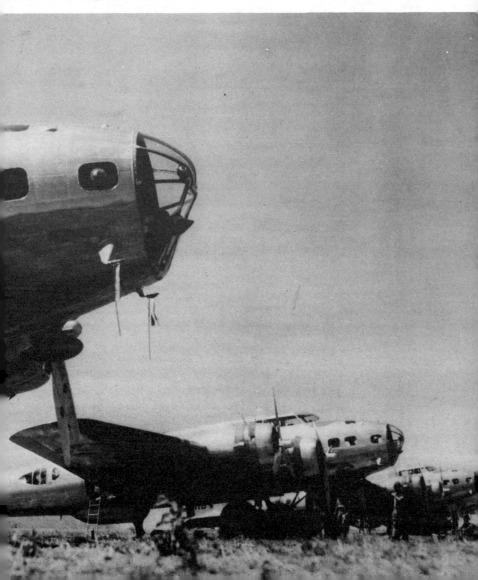

the ground by a strafing Zero. The
other three pilots escaped, either by
parachute or crash-landing, one of
them, Lieutenant McMahon, re-
marking later that he took off under
three Zeros and that 'I had them
just where they wanted me.' His
undercarriage stayed down, his plane
had been hit, yet he made the climb to
the clouds, attacked a dive-bomber
and killed its gunner, was out of
ammunition when he attacked a Zero

with his engine on fire, bailed out to
be shot at again while hanging in
his parachute. He finally landed on
the edge of the bay, among the croco-
dile-infested mangroves where he
was eventually rescued by a motor
launch.

When Lieutenant Rice bailed out
he too was shot at by a Zero pilot but
survived to drop safely in a swamp.
And Lieutenant Glover attacked the
Zero attacking Rice until his own

The fast, clean lines of the P-40

plane was also attacked and damaged, and he dived away down to the ground where he crash-landed violently, his Kittyhawk breaking up in a scattered wreck from which nevertheless he was able to walk away. Darwin's courageous little fighter force was destroyed, and so too were six Hudsons, three Catalinas, the Liberator and the Beechcraft transports.

In Darwin Harbour there was a wide assortment of vessels for the enemy to choose as targets – altogether forty-seven, ranging from twelve-ton patrol boats up to a 12,000-ton transport. There were two sloops and five corvettes of the RAN, as well as a destroyer and a seaplane tender of the USN among the numerous naval vessels, and there were eleven merchant ships, four of which had formed the Timor convoy.

Above : Kittyhawk in level flight. *Below :* Now repossessed by 5th Air Force airmen, this machine was captured and used by the Japanese for flight and combat tests

At a wharf the *Neptuna* was unloading a cargo of depth-charges when the sirens sounded two ·minutes before 10am. By 10.30am the formations of enemy aircraft had turned to seaward and ten minutes later the all-clear was sounded. At noon, Darwin was raided again.

After making a rendezvous at Palau the Japanese 1st Carrier Division which included the *Akagi* and *Kaga* and 2nd Carrier Division with the *Hiryu* and *Soryu* had moved from Staring Bay and entered the Banda Sea on 18th February to support the Timor invading forces. Although the Allied naval forces based at Darwin were not considered to be of great danger to the invasion, fighter and dive-bomber traffic had been observed flying from Darwin through Timor, and Nagumo was asked to lend his sledgehammer force to crack the Darwin nut. Aircrews from his carriers had proved their highly trained skill, their accuracy with high-level pattern bombing, dive-bombing and fighter strafing at Pearl Harbor. The second raiding force of bombers flew in from Kendari and Ambon in the Celebes. Nagumo's planes attacked first, Commander Fuchida leading a flight of twenty-seven Kate bombers at 14,000 feet, followed by a large flight of Val dive-bombers and thirty-six Zeros. The fifty-four land-based bombers from the 1st Attack Force were two formations of twin-engined Bettys.

Including one Zero crash-landed on Melville Island where the pilot was taken prisoner by aborigines, the Japanese losses (an estimated five shot down and five damaged, accounted for by P-40s and anti-aircraft fire) were negligible compared with the havoc created on the harbour, the wharves and at the RAAF station. Five merchant ships, including the 12,000-ton *Meigs*, were sunk, three were beached and two were damaged. The *Neptuna* blew up at her wharf and on another wharf a group of waterside workers, who had just knocked off work for their ten o'clock 'smoke-oh', had no time to take shelter before a bomb landed nearby, killing twenty-one of them and hurling a railway engine into the sea. The main RAAF aerodrome was plastered in both raids. During the second, observers noticed that the two flights of Betty bombers approached from opposite directions in wide curves; where they met, it seemed, they released their bombs to accurately pattern the field and buildings with exploding bombs. Two hangars, the main store and other buildings were destroyed. The total death roll of seamen, servicemen and civilians, including several aborigines, was about 260, and 150 were wounded; the post-raid calculations of casualties was confused by the numbers taken on, and off, the hospital ship *Manunda* which was not spared, receiving a direct hit forward of the bridge.

Pearl Harbor and Port Darwin were later avenged for these carrier raids: on 4th June Nagumo's four carriers and many of his highly trained, irreplaceable aircrews were destroyed by Admiral Nimitz's pilots at the famous Midway battle.

The trend of events in the Philippines, Malaya and the NEI led Australians to expect invasion on their northern shores, and the Darwin raid had far-reaching effects, both on the morale of the civilian population and the planning for defence of the country. It was a time of indecision for both political and military leaders, when it was possible that the bulk of war material would be diverted to the effort in China and India. Wavell was instructed by the Combined Chiefs of Staff to defend Java to the last, a hopeless task as Wavell saw it, preferring to concentrate on making Burma and Australia secure. The Chiefs in Washington asked him to withdraw his ABDA Command headquarters and hand over the troops in Java to the original Dutch command. Wavell recommended that as the ABDA Command could serve no

Timor Commandos. *Left :* **In the mountains of Mindelo, Timor**
Above : **Posing at headquarters**

further useful purpose it should be dissolved and so it was, on 25th February. The Dutch commander, General ter Poorten, possessed then a relatively strong army of about 32,000 men and a naval force, under Admiral Helfrich, of eight cruisers, twelve destroyers and thirty-two submarines. But the combined Allied air force was only about one sixth the strength of the Japanese aircraft available for their invasion.

The Allies' greatest need in Java was for fighters and there was some confusion about the allocation of 198 of the precious planes delivered to Australia during January. Even Wavell assumed that the bulk of them were being held back for Australian defence but the truth was that they were lost before they could be flown into battle: fifty-nine on the *Langley* and *Seawitch* and forty-four on ferrying flights to Java; fifty-five arrived in Australia too late for assembly and transport to the island; thirty-eight were delivered. On 27th February the Japanese invaded Java and after a series of sea, land and air battles in a despair of disorganisation and hopelessness, the Allies surrendered on 9th March. Kittyhawk pilots had scored some successes against Zeros before being shot down or destroyed on the ground by the overwhelming enemy air strength.

While Java was falling to the Japanese, the North Western Area of Australia continued to suffer raids from enemy aircraft. A few hundred miles south-west along the coast from Darwin is the small pearling township of Broome, then a stopping point for flying-boat traffic from the northern islands, and especially busy

Above : Oil tanks blaze in the devastating attack on Darwin
Right : Firemen fighting the inferno have to use asbestos shields

with flights to and from Java. The Qantas Empire flying-boat *Circe* was shot down on its homeward flight on 27th February and the controllers of the base expected the inevitable raid. RAAF and civilian Short flying-boats and Dutch Dorniers and Catalinas used the deep-water anchorage or rested on the bottom of the bay when the tide, which rose and fell as much as thirty feet, was out. If the Japanese had raided on 2nd March, the day they made their preliminary reconnaissance, there would have been only three flying-boats moored, but four alighted in the evening and nine more arrived during the night. The captains of these aircraft were informed of the reconnaissance and expected raid yet they were still there soon after breakfast the following morning when nine Zeros flew in, low across the harbour entrance, and shot up every flying-boat. The raiders also attacked the Broome aerodrome where they destroyed two Flying Fortresses, a Liberator and three other aircraft on the ground, and shot down in flames a second Liberator which had just taken off. On the way back to their base the Zero pilots met and shot down a Dutch DC-3 which carried a valuable consignment of diamonds with it into the sea. At Broome one Zero may have been fatally hit by a Dutch gunner who blistered his arm while supporting an aircraft machine gun with which he fired at the planes. The Japanese may have suffered this one casualty, but the aircraft loss to the Allies was twenty-four, and an estimated seventy people, civilians and servicemen, lost their lives.

Kittyhawks were urgently needed to defend Darwin and the thinly-

populated, isolated ports along the long stretches of coast, However, it wasn't until after Java fell that the 9th, the first of three squadrons of the 49th Pursuit Group USAAF, arrived, led by Lieutenant-Colonel Paul B Wurtsmith, on 17th March. Before these P-40s arrived there had been several other raids. A petrol dump and a light aircraft had been destroyed on the airfield at Wyndham and an old ship, which had previously been weakened in a bombing raid at sea, sank alongside the wharf. Darwin was raided on 4th March by eight Zeros and by another ten on the 10th; a squadron of bombers attacked the RAAF station six days later, causing few casualties and slight damage to one Hudson. Although there were not many worthwhile targets left, the Japanese lost an opportunity to raid heavily and more frequently before

more fighters were sent to Darwin.

There was every indication that an invasion on the north west coast would take place, if not on a large scale then at least by a commando to wreck installations and attack the local defences. Two battalions of an experienced AIF brigade, recently returned from the Middle East, had moved to the Darwin area but before they arrived the military defences rested with partly-trained militiamen. The need for AIF men was desperate, judging by the report issued by the Central War Room on 24th March: 'Recent Intelligence indicates the concentration of five aircraft-carriers in the Celebes area, including two new arrivals from Japan; also the presence of a number of military landing craft and a probable landing-craft carrier at Koupang. This ... with air raids on the northern part of

A killer's career finished. Zero in the hands of Allied Intelligence; Port Moresby, April 1942

Australia and information of an operation timed for the end of the month, gives indications that an attack on Australia from the Netherlands East Indies may occur by the end of the month.' Wurtsmith's Kittyhawks were ready, patrolling the coast and protecting shipping. The P-40s made their first interception when nine bombers attacked Katherine, 180 miles inland, where the only casualties were one aborigine killed and another wounded. The following day, the 23rd, the Kittyhawks were too far away to intercept a bombing and strafing raid on Wyndham's aerodrome.

That the Japanese were not planning a large-scale invasion was indicated by the size of the air raids, which were made by small numbers of aircraft, suggesting a purpose of armed reconnaissance only over the north-west area, keeping watch on developments and bombing suitable targets on the

way. The two other Kittyhawk squadrons arrived during April. The pilots intercepted seven raids between 28th March and 27th April, demonstrating their skill by shooting down fifteen bombers and eleven fighters and scoring on six probables. Eight Kittyhawks were shot down but only three pilots were lost. These raids caused few casualties and little damage on the ground. New fighter strips were constructed beside straight stretches of the main Darwin highway and dispersal areas were cleared among the tall eucalyptus. The few remaining RAAF Hudson bombers also hit back at the Japanese, bombing airfields and ports at Kupang, Ambon and Dili. The bombers also dropped supplies to Australian commandos operating in the Timor bushland.

Improved radar facilities gave early warning of raids so that on some occasions the pilots were able to climb to a suitable attacking height before the Japanese bombers and their Zero escorts arrived. The Americans were well trained and were quick to

conditions on the strip, the seals blown off in the first firing. Living conditions were hard and monotonous in the dry heat, but although there were myriads of flies and mosquitoes, there were none of the tropical diseases such as malaria, dengue and scrub typhus that were prevalent in New Guinea.

By the end of April the situation at Darwin had changed from confusion and near-panic to confidence in the army and air force should the expected invasion take place. The lull which developed after the shooting down of eleven raiders lasted until the end of July, providing a respite for the fighters while the bombers extended their operations. The Japanese flew back over Darwin on 25th July and every day until the 30th, flying too high for the Kittyhawks to reach them, except during the second raid on the last day when about forty-five bombers and fighters were intercepted, the Americans shooting down six Zeros and two bombers, and scoring six probables and five damaged.

Between March and the end of August the 49th Fighter Group had shot down a total of sixty-four enemy bombers and fighters for the loss in action of only sixteen P-40s. General Royce, USAAF, later observed that credit should be given the 49th Group for twice that number of enemy aircraft shot down, for many of the Japanese planes were undoubtedly lost in the 500-mile flight over water back to their base, as a result of mechanical failure, lack of fuel, and damage sustained in combat.

A USAAF study made later found that operations in the South West Pacific Area has 'definitely proven that a pilot left in the combat area for any length of time (for example, thirty days of intense action) is a casualty.' This did not apply to the Darwin area where the action was not so severe but in Port Moresby there were periods of combat likely to strain the nerves of the toughest fighter pilot.

learn how to adapt the proven tactics of the AVG pilots; flying in sections of pairs for higher manoeuvrability and better protection against being bounced, diving to attack and continuing down with the Kittyhawk's faster diving speed to leave the Zero behind, and not attempting to dogfight with the faster climbing and quicker turning enemy plane. With early warning allowing the P-40s to reach a suitable height, these tactics, plus the skill and determination of the P-40 pilots, enabled them to shoot down eleven enemy aircraft without loss on 25th April, an outstanding success for P-40s in those days. Another reason for this victory was the careful maintenance of aircraft and armament by ground crews. Every third night the .50-inch machine guns were taken out of the aircraft wings and completely stripped, oiled and polished so that gun failure in combat was reduced to a minimum. Ammunition in the gun belts was also taken out, each round oiled and cleaned of dust before being re-belted. Gun ports were sealed against the dusty

Defence of
Port Moresby

As the Japanese invaded island after island in their southern advance the Allies had made many decisions to stand and fight: to hold Singapore, Bataan, Java and other points along the thousands of sea miles the enemy was traversing so rapidly and successfully. One of these stand-and-fight decisions was also made for Port Moresby, regardless of the fact that there was no strong force of infantry, no artillery of any consequence, few anti-aircraft guns and only a small RAAF force of six Catalina flying-boats and seven Hudsons. Patrolling the enormous area of the eastern approaches to Australia and New Zealand was left to a squadron of Allied cruisers, *HMAS Australia, USS Chicago, HMNZS Achilles* and *HMNZS Leander*, and two USN destroyers.

The Japanese were as determined to capture Port Moresby as the Allies were to hold the base which was strategically important to both, being on the southern side of the New Guinea peninsula overlooking Torres Strait and a convenient distance from Rabaul where the Japanese were developing their prize into a large naval and air base. Their activities were observed by aerial reconnaissance and the Allied cruisers were prepared to intercept any seaborne approach down past the Solomons towards Australia. On 20th February Vice-Admiral Wilson Brown's carrier *USS Lexington* and support ships joined the Allied squadron for a planned attack on Rabaul but a more satisfactory – to the Allies – air battle over the sea took place instead. Grumman F4F Wildcats, the stubby manoeuvrable US Navy fighters shot down two of three Mavis four-engined flying-boats in a morning interception and during the afternoon the Wildcats made history: they fought the first battle between carrier-borne aircraft and won hands down, destroying

twelve of the enemy for the loss of only two Wildcats and one pilot.

The enemy effort was slow to begin, compared with their earlier projects, but was to develop into an elaborate plan of direct invasion by sea, a cross-country march and the seizure of Milne Bay for use as an advanced base on the Papuan extremity. For the first time in the war, the conquering Japanese were to be stopped and beaten back – the seaborne invasion foiled by the US Navy, the Japanese army defeated by a comparatively small force of Australian soldiers in the Papuan mountains and at Milne Bay, while Kittyhawk fighters fought off enemy planes and supported the infantry with machine guns and bombs.

The American naval interception which resulted in the Battle of the Coral Sea, south east of Papua and south west of the Solomons, has been fully described elsewhere. The Japanese transports, carriers and support ships were in the Coral Sea as a result of Admiral Yamamoto's order: 'The South Sea Force and the Navy will occupy Port Moresby; the Navy will occupy Tulagi and Deboyne Island; they will establish bases and strengthen air operations against Australia. Another unit will occupy Nauru and Ocean Islands to secure phosphates.' Rear-Admiral Fletcher's carriers *Yorktown* and *Lexington*, with their supporting cruisers and destroyers, had first moved into the area after Tulagi Island in the Solomons was lost on 4th May. Fletcher had raided the Japanese there, sinking and damaging several ships, before moving on to join Rear-Admiral Crace's Australian squadron. On the morning of 7th May Japanese carrier-borne planes attacked and sank the US destroyer *Sims* and fatally damaged the tanker *Neosho*. Crace's ships were sent off to intercept the Japanese invasion convoy on their expected route while his scouting planes searched for enemy carriers. The *Shoho* was discovered

35

Crew leaps from the *Lexington* after the explosion which spelled her end

and sunk, along with all her aircraft, by the attack force from both American carriers. Crace's ships were attacked, unsuccessfully, by Japanese torpedo-carrying aircraft, five of which were shot down, and shortly afterwards his ships were again attacked, also unsuccessfully, by nineteen American bombers which mistook the ships for the Japanese invasion convoy.

The following morning the carrier-versus-carrier battle continued. In this second round the *Yorktown* was superficially damaged by a direct hit and a near-miss, but the *Lexington* was hit by two bombs and two torpedoes. She kept going, however, until internal explosions sealed her fate and she was abandoned and sunk. American pilots scored damaging strikes on the *Shokaku* and the final result was one carrier sunk and one damaged on both sides, and the *Sims* and *Neosho* lost. For the Allies it was nevertheless a resounding victory: the invasion of Port Moresby from the sea was cancelled. Every year Australians celebrate the victory with a festival called Coral Sea Week.

Another factor which contributed to the eventual security of Moresby was the sporadic bombing of Rabaul by RAAF, USAAF and USN aircraft, delaying early Japanese plans to land in New Guinea, at Buna.

The aircraft needs at Port Moresby in March amounted to at least twenty squadrons of fighters, bombers, dive-bombers, torpedo-bombers, transports, flying-boats and army co-operation planes, needs that were quite impossible to satisfy from the resources available. There were, however, more Kittyhawks arriving in Australia to fill the order for over 700 required by the RAAF. America was the only feasible source of supply for fighter aircraft with Britain hard pressed to supply her air forces in the Middle East and India, and the long sealanes of the Pacific and Indian Oceans were too dangerous without strong escorts; warships needed for these duties were busy elsewhere. P-40s and P-39 Aira-cobras were being shipped to China, Russia, the Middle East and Britain as well as to Australia. RAAF and USAAF staff preferred the P-40 for their squadrons in the SWPA despite the early feelings of hopelessness expressed by pilots in their inability to outclimb and out-manoeuvre the enemy. The AVG and Wurtsmith's pilots had proved that by using suitable tactics the Zero's superior qualities could be overcome. Early in 1942 the P-40 was the only suitable fighter available in the quantities required although increasing numbers of P-39s were to be sent out. General Kenney, who was later to command the US Fifth Air Force, later described the P-40 as a fighter that 'could slug it out, absorb gun fire and fly home, while the Zero burns or falls apart as soon as it is touched'. Time after time P-40s flew home with airframe damage that would have been fatal to Zeros.

Instead of the twenty squadrons of aircraft needed for various purposes, Moresby was to get one squadron of Kittyhawks. Without its belly tank the P-40 could carry a 1,000-pound bomb load, increased from an original load of six fifty-pound bombs, as well as 1,200 rounds of .50-inch ammunition for its six guns. Belly tanks were however usually carried, even on short-range operations, and the plane flew initially on this supplementary fuel, switching over to the normal internal supply and dropping the belly tank either when it was empty or before if there was action. The internal supply of 148 gallons gave a maximum range of 350 miles, including half an hour of combat at full throttle. Remarkably, the tankers maintained a good supply of aviation spirit to the fighters at Moresby, and there were sufficient reserves. By March Australia had a fuel reserve of 10,000,000 gallons, brought in from America and the Far East. It was found that the American blends gave a slight increase in efficiency over the Eastern fuels because of their greater heating value and by causing less distortion to carburettor diaphrams.

Japanese daylight bombing of Port Moresby began on 3rd February, when twenty-one bombs were dropped from a few raiding aircraft. By the 28th the Japanese were more venturesome, sending eleven bombers escorted by Zeros to attack the Catalina base where three of the flying-boats were destroyed and a fourth damaged. The air force strength on that evening was one Hudson and two Catalinas. 'Photo Joe' was active all the time over the port as well as over airfields and small towns on the northern Papuan coast across the Owen Stanley mountains. Japanese troops landed at two of these hut-built towns, Lae and Salamaua, on 8th March, and the small garrison of local volunteers and RAAF radiomen withdrew to the hills – the only sensible thing to do. From then on Japanese activity along this part of the coast was observed by a unique team of New Guinea volunteers, the Coastwatchers, who were to render highly valuable services here and in other parts of New Guinea and the Solomons, operating in enemy territory with only a few reliable natives to assist them and guard against approaching enemy search parties. The rest of the white civilian population of New Guinea had been evacuated; over 2,000 men, women and children were taken south in a fleet of battered old Ford monoplanes, two-seater Moths, Dragon biplanes, DC-3s and bombers.

In the emergency that arose after the Japanese advance in the East, some experienced Australian fighter pilots had been recalled from Britain and the Middle East. They would be the nucleus of new squadrons to be formed with pilots just finishing their training. When the first twenty-five Kittyhawks were made available to the RAAF at the end of February a new squadron, 75, was quickly formed at Townsville, the closest major air base to New Guinea. Supervising the formation and training of the squadron was Squadron Leader Peter Jeffrey DSO, DFC, who had been a squadron and wing leader of P-40 fighters in the Western Desert. In nine days the new squadron completed a quick course of gunnery, formation flying and battle tactics before leaving for Moresby. Two weeks after its formation Squadron Leader J F Jackson

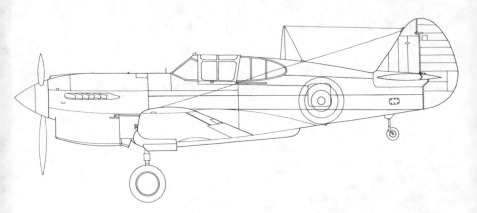

Curtiss P-40E (RAF Kittyhawk II)
Engine : Allison V-1710-39, 1,150hp. *Armament :* six .50-inch machine guns plus one
500lb and two 100lb bombs. *Maximum speed :* 362mph at 15,000 feet
Climb : 20,000 feet in 11.5 minutes. *Ceiling :* 29,000 feet. *Range :* 850 miles
Weight empty/loaded : 6,350lbs/9,200lbs. *Span :* 37 feet 4 inches
Length : 31 feet 2 inches

who had been appointed to its command, led his seventeen Kittyhawks on the long flight via Cooktown and Horn Island to Moresby. Jackson, who was thirty-four years old and known as 'Old John', was a Queensland farmer who had also fought in the Western Desert during 1941. Another member of the squadron was Flight-Lieutenant Leslie Jackson, brother of the leader.

The arrival of the P-40s– 'Tomorrowhawks' or 'Mythhawks' as the troops at Moresby called the fighters which had been promised for so long – surprised the anti-aircraft gunners, who were accustomed to seeing only Japanese single-engined aircraft approaching Seven Mile Drome, the main airstrip inland from the town. The gunners' reaction was to open fire, accurate enough to damage three of four aircraft which Peter Jeffrey had led in, a bullet just missing his head as he was landing.

The Kittyhawks' 'mythical' presence was destroyed about one hour after their arrival when two of the fighters, piloted by Flying Officers Wackett and Cox, were scrambled to intercept a Japanese twin-engined reconnaissance plane. They caught up with it at 10,000 feet and shot it down; it blew up before diving into the sea at the entrance to the reef. The garrison militiamen, keen but inexperienced, their morale not at all helped by the news bulletins which contained only lists of withdrawals and defeats, and by being separated from Australia by the wide sea and with no naval or air support in sight, were now heartened by the arrival of 75 Squadron; as the Japanese plane dived into the sea the troops cheered. They even apologised for shooting at the fighters.

Before the Japanese could discover that there were fighters at Seven Mile, the Australians decided to raid the enemy aerodrome at Lae where reconnaissance photographs showed attractive targets of lined-up fighters and bombers – the over-confident enemy was making the same dispersal mistake as the Allies had made when they felt secure against air attack and tidy-minded station commanders had marshalled their planes in ranks. Jackson led a flight of five on the strafing attack, approaching from seaward and diving through cloud. In two runs they set alight twelve and damaged another five enemy planes. On their first run across the aerodrome three of the P-40s strafed a line of a dozen Zeros practically at ground level, Flying Officer Piper making his run so low that his Kittyhawk flicked a wingtip against one of the parked Japanese fighters.

Flight-Lieutenant Turnbull led another flight as top cover protection to the strafers, tackling a standing patrol of Zeros sighted at 10,000 feet. Some of these which had dived to attack the strafers were chased by Wackett who engaged them in a dogfight; his engine was set on fire and he was forced to ditch his plane in the sea. The remaining Zeros in the air were engaged by the rest of Turnbull's flight and two Zeros were shot down, one by Turnbull and one by Flying Officer Pettett. Flight-Lieutenant Anderson, who had flown one of the Wirraways in the futile defensive flight at Rabaul, was shot down and failed to return. However, Wackett did return, after some days. He had inflated his Mae West, and floating and swimming through shark-infested water (he saw several swim past) after nine hours crawled onto the beach near a native village. Because the Melanesians in Japanese territory had been threatened with reprisals for any kind of anti-Japanese behaviour, and some had already been executed, it was a gamble whether a shot-down airman would be aided to escape or handed over to the Japanese who had no qualms about beheading prisoners, especially pilots: this form of brutality was perpetrated many times during the course of the war in New Guinea. Fortunately for Wackett the tribe who found him risked reprisals, as other tribes were to do on numerous other occasions, and he was led to the New Guinea Volunteers' camp, walking bare-foot over the rough country, and from there walked in borrowed boots most of the way back to Port Moresby.

It was altogether a bad day for the Japanese at Lae. Two Hudsons also visited the aerodrome, and although their bombing was ineffectual, their gunners shot down two Zeros. Four Flying Fortresses from Townsville arrived after the Hudsons, scored a direct hit on an ammunition dump and destroyed two more aircraft. And it was a glorious day for the Allies who had long suffered the ignominy of inadequate defence against enemy planes which had made sixteen raids in comparative safety against Moresby, and could have smashed the place to a shambles. The hitting back had begun with a loss to the Japanese of seventeen aircraft and another six severely damaged; the presence of one Kittyhawk squadron had completely altered their position.

From the point of view of flying quality, the Japanese had the better fighter. It was more manoeuvrable, had a much higher rate of climb and a service ceiling over 3,000 feet higher than that of the P-40E Kittyhawk. Because it had two 20mm cannon to supplement its two 7.7mm machine guns, the Zero was better armed than the P-40 with its six .50-inch machine guns. Compared with the P-40's range of 650 miles on internal fuel the range of the Zero was 1,000 miles, which was one of the contributing factors to its success in the campaigns in China, Malaya, the Philippines and the Pacific, where long-range bomber escorts and fighter strikes caused so much destruction to Allied aircraft.

To counter these advantages, the Kittyhawk was faster, at 15,000 feet, by about 25mph; its armour and sturdier construction allowed it to absorb much more punishment and in a dive the heavier and more powerful Kittyhawk was much the faster plane.

The Allison V-1710-39 twelve-cylinder liquid-cooled engine provided 1,150hp at 15,000 feet, compared with the Nakajima Sakae 12 twin-row radial and its constant rating of 950hp up to 14,000 feet. The Kittyhawk's best rate of climb was 2,100 feet per minute at 5,000 feet, the Zero's was over 1,000 feet faster; the A6M3 Zero produced late in 1942 could climb at 4,500 feet per minute.

A complete history of the Zero can be found in another Ballantine book but a brief description of the background of the Kittyhawk's major opponent in New Guinea should be given here. It was the second production model of the Mitsubishi fighter, the Navy's Type O Carrier Model 11, the Mitsubishi Heavy Industry Company's A6M2, *Rei Sentoki* (Zero Fighter) nicknamed *Reisen* by its pilots and code-named Zeke by the

RAAF Beaufort begins bombing mission against Japanese positions

Allies, although Allied pilots continued to refer to it by its original Allied designation, Zero, for most of the war. The Nakajima Army fighter, the Ki-43 *Hayabusa*, code named Oscar, was similar in appearance but had a lower performance.

The Zero's designer, Jiro Horikoshi, had gone straight to the heart of the aircraft designing craft, paring metal to give a high power-to-weight ratio. The highest security precautions surrounded its development and the first flight of the A6M1 took place in April 1939. Twelve months before Japan entered the war the A6M2 began flight trials, its range for the strike role and for bomber escort, and general performance proving it to be the world's best all-round fighter except for one factor – its vulnerability. In its first encounter with twenty-seven obsolete Chinese aircraft all were shot down by thirteen Zeros. This and later successes of the amazing Zero were reported by Claire

Chennault to the Air Service in Washington, where the information was filed and stayed unopened in its file when war broke out against Japan. The pilots who were to fight the Zero had no idea of its abilities and were, in fact, led to believe that it was not much more than a hotted-up sports plane.

Along with its new warplane industry the Japanese navy and army bred a group of pilots who were as highly trained and thoroughly dedicated as any of the world's best airmen. In 1940, when the best British and German fighters could stay in the air for about four hours with auxiliary fuel, Zeros were staying up for twelve, their patient pilots skilfully controlling and experimenting with pitch control and fuel supply to get the best possible endurance out of their machines. Such dedication and devotion of the men to their planes gave Japan a stronger air arm than mere numbers could have provided. The eventual loss of the skilled pilots and their replacement by others fresh from air training schools speeded the decimation of Japan's air force. There was little promotion incentive for these aces from the China and early Pacific campaigns. Petty Officer Sakai, the first Japanese fighter pilot to shoot down a P-40 in the Philippines, and the first to shoot down a Flying Fortress, was still a Petty Officer in 1942, at Lae. (In fact, it was virtually impossible in the Japanese armed forces to rise from non-commissioned to commissioned rank.) There he was with other representatives of the best of his navy's fighter pilots, some of whom had been constantly on active service, and reinforcements who were chosen for the Lae hot-spot went there because of the high standard of their flying. A more formidable group than the Lae Wing would have been hard to find and constant fighting kept them on their mettle.

In his book *Samurai*, Sakai describes the Lae airfield, originally scraped out of the tropical growth for prewar transports carrying gold from the Bulolo goldfields to Moresby, and for other light aircraft which carried passengers to various New Guinea settlements: 'I groaned when I circled the field. Where were the hangars, the maintenance shops, the control tower? Where was anything but a dirty, small runway? I felt as though I were landing on a carrier deck. On three sides of the runway there towered the rugged mountains of the Papuan peninsula; the fourth side, from which I approached, was bordered by the ocean.' Their command post had curtains for walls, three vehicles including the fuel tanker were their only transport and twenty-three pilots and other NCOs shared a single shack, their only quarters, with candles their only illumination. Life at the base was monotonous and dull, and their food rations comprised mainly rice, soybeans, canned meat, fruit juice and candy. Replacement aircraft, pilots and supplies were flown in from Rabaul or brought by ship or submarine.

The Japanese possessed no early warning radar system, and their anti-aircraft defences were manned by 200 naval ratings. Another hundred men maintained the planes for thirty pilots. From the pilots' point of view, Sakai records, there was no tougher fighting than at Lae:

'Early in April, thirty of us from the Tainan Wing transferred to a new air base at Lae, on the eastern coast of New Guinea. Captain Masahisa Saito led our group to the new installation. Then began some of the fiercest air battles of the entire Pacific war. Only 180 miles away from the Allied bastion of Port Moresby, we began our new assignments by flying escort almost daily for our bombers, which flew from Rabaul to hammer the enemy installations in the critical Moresby area. No longer was the war entirely one-sided. As often as we lashed out at Moresby, Allied bombers and fighters came to attack Lae. The valour of the

Allied pilots and their willingness to fight surprised us all. Whenever they attacked Lae, they were invariably intercepted and several of their planes were damaged or shot down. Our attacks on Moresby also contributed to the Allied losses.

'The willingness of the Allied pilots to engage us in combat deserves special mention here, for, regardless of the odds, their fighters were always screaming in to attack. And it is important to point out that their fighter planes were clearly inferior in performance to our own Zeros. Furthermore, almost all of our pilots were skilled air veterans: coupled with the Zero's outstanding performance, this afforded us a distinct advantage. The men we fought then were among the bravest I have ever encountered, no less so than our own pilots who, three years later, went out willingly on missions from which there was no hope of return.'

Japanese retaliation to the visitation of Kittyhawks, Hudsons and Fortresses on 22nd March was made the following day; nineteen bombers from Rabaul approached too high for the P-40s to reach them before they dropped their bombs ineffectively on the runway. Four avenging Zeros from Lae fared better, shooting up two P-40s bogged in wet ground away from their dispersal bays, and damaging a third. One Zero was shot down by ground fire. The following day Piper shot down a reconnaissance bomber and Lance Jackson shot down a Zero escorting eighteen bombers which made their run but also caused little damage.

Although the Australians had the

Left: Bell Airacobra skids in to belly landing. *Above:* Scramble on Guadalcanal

use of a radar station, the high mountains, separating the base from Lae, limited its value to scanning the sea approaches. The few observer posts in the Owen Stanley mountains were spread over a one-hundred-mile radius; they functioned efficiently at times yet more often than not their reports arrived too late for the Kittyhawks to climb to interception altitude. The climate at Moresby was generally drier than at Lae but the monsoon rains fell in March and aircraft at Seven Mile sometimes bogged in the soft ground off the main runway which was uncompleted by 400 yards.

There were accidents, regular events on most airfields where new pilots were sometimes careless, and even the most experienced were likely to be involved in fatal collisions. Three of the fighters being delivered from Brisbane, where the squadron had formed, were lost in crashes. After three days of operations another seven had been destroyed by enemy action and in accidents. Repairing planes in the conditions existing at Moresby was very trying to the maintenance crews sweating in the heat to keep the Kittyhawks flying. Some essential tools were in short supply and instead of waiting for official supplies to trickle through from the south, some mechanics unofficially 'borrowed' from American neighbours while they were away in shelters during air raids. Compared with the living conditions in the Japanese camp, the Australians were much better off – their service rations were of a higher standard, their quarters were almost reasonable, medical services were efficient and there was some security in the fact that there were rapidly expanding bases behind them. There were, however, the same tropical diseases to guard against and some of the pilots soon went down with dengue fever. These casualties were only temporary, for the fever usually lasted only a few days, but extra work was given to the fit pilots who were rostered for stand-by duty and early morning patrols which began before 0500hrs. Generally they had quieter nights than the Japanese whose sleep was disturbed with greater frequency as the Allies mounted increasing numbers of day and night raids on the Lae Wing.

The Allied air forces and armies were being marshalled in a programme of expansion while the Chiefs of Staff still expected not only the New Guinea invasions – they also prepared to repel assaults anywhere along the eastern, northern and western coasts. US General Brett was given overall command of the air and General Sir Thomas Blamey command of the land forces under General Douglas MacArthur, who flew from Mindanao and landed at Batchelor airstrip, Darwin, on 17th March, to take up his appointment as Supreme Commander of armed forces in the SWPA. Allied Air Force Headquarters were established in Melbourne; training, maintenance and aircraft depots were planned for the expansion of increasing numbers of aircrews and the reception of aircraft being delivered from American and Australian factories. An Australian-built fighter had been ingeniously designed for manufacturers from local facilities when it seemed likely that the country would be cut off from outside help. The CA-12 Boomerang was designed around the most powerful engine available, a Pratt and Whitney Twin Wasp 1,200hp motor which gave it a top speed of 296mph at 7,600 feet, and many Wirraway components. The first one was completed fourteen weeks after the design was approved, and although it was no match for

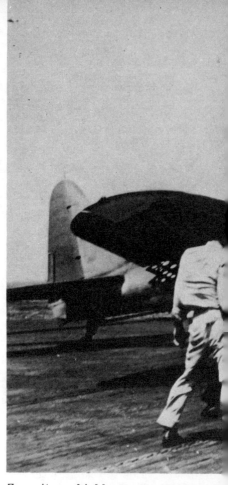

Zeros it was highly manoeuvrable and suitable for army co-operation work in photo-reconnaissance and in ground strafing, using its two 20mm cannon and four .303-inch Browning machine guns. The British Beaufort torpedo bomber was also in the process of being produced in Australia. With the numbers of fighters, bombers and other service aircraft ordered in Britain and America, the future air strength was formidable but in April 1942 it was still a paper tiger. The increase in army strength was more real with the return of seasoned AIF men from the Middle East and the strengthening of the Militia. The troops were armed with locally produced munitions.

Early in April the Kittyhawks at Moresby were given the extra task of escorting Dauntless dive-bombers of the US 8th Squadron in attacks on Lae. More suited to operating from aircraft-carriers, the Dauntlesses soon became unserviceable in the rough conditions at Port Moresby and of the fourteen written off during their two-month stay only two were lost in action. Heavy B-17s and medium B-25s and B-26s staged through Moresby strips on various missions, covered on short-range journeys by the Kittyhawks. Sometimes 75 Squadron were down in numbers due to losses and unserviceability and the bombers were left unescorted: on one occasion five B-25 Mitchells were

Kittyhawks escorting Dauntless dive-bombers fought off the Zeros defending Lae

shot down and one badly damaged when eight of the bombers attacked the Lae base. Until the promised American squadrons of P-39 Airacobras arrived to relieve them, 75 Squadron continued their private war with Captain Saito's wing and combat over Lae or Moresby occurred daily during most of April. A raid on one base brought a quick reply from the other, tactics on both sides continually varying in order to win a victory. The squadron had been offered a respite at the end of March but Jackson pleaded to stay; the pilots'

47

morale was high and they were keen to fight on regardless of the incidence of malaria and dengue fever in the camp and the long thirst for bottles of Foster's lager.

During operations – attacking enemy aircraft in the air and on the ground, shooting up supply dumps and anti-aircraft positions – Jackson was shot down on two occasions. The Kitty-hawks were almost always out-numbered by at least three or four to one and flew into action with a height disadvantage. On 6th April, fire from two enemy bombers, which he had attacked and damaged, disabled his P-40 and forced him down to a belly-landing on a coral reef near Moresby. Les Jackson, who was flying that day with his brother, dropped a life-jacket to the squadron leader who returned to land unharmed. Four days later John Jackson was on a lone reconnaissance over Lae when he was jumped by three Zeros. Turning into them his guns jammed after firing a brief burst at one of the Zeros, then another hit his P-40 with cannon shells. Jackson managed to ditch his plane in the sea half-way between Lae and Salamaua, but he was still under attack so he scrambled out of the cockpit and feigned death by floating inert in the water. When the Zeros flew off, two natives waded out to assist him ashore then led him to their village where his fate was debated. His two helpers did not stay for the result and took to the jungle with the bare-footed pilot – flying boots would fill with water and were always kicked off by pilots ditching or parachuting into the sea. Reaching the Bulolo camp after an eight-day painful march over the rough country and past Japanese patrols, Jackson was carried to Wau and flown out by one of the Dauntlesses, escorted by a P-40. 'Old John' was nearly home when

Above left: RAAF Lockheed Hudson bombers. *Left:* The Australian home product – the CA12 Boomerang, invaluable on straffing missions

49

three Zeros attacked the Dauntless as it made its landing approach. The escort tried desperately to intercept but the Zeros avoided it and one fired a burst at the Dauntless whose pilot, Lieutenant V A Schwab, skilfully took such evasive action that he was able to land on another strip. The Zero had, however, scored; the Dauntless was holed and Jackson lost the tip off his right index finger.

On 11th April the Kittyhawks escorted the dive-bombers on a successful fuel and ammunition dump exploding fray, meeting a large swarm of Zeros over the target, shooting down four for the loss of a forced-down Kittyhawk whose pilot was captured and 'died' a few weeks later, the same fate falling to the two crew members of a Dauntless also downed during the attack. A few P-39s had arrived for local experience at Moresby and Saburo Sakai records that on 11th April nine Zeros led by Lieutenant Sasai scouted over Moresby in three 'Vee' formations. The Japanese fighting tactics were to fly sections of three planes in a staggered formation: number two about one-hundred yards behind the leader and number three another one-hundred yards further away, both wingmen weaving as they kept watch for enemy aircraft. When they sighted the opposition they endeavoured to box individual aircraft, one on either side and one behind, firing bursts up to ten seconds as they took turns to get into the firing position behind. They were usually inaccurate at long range firing on Allied aircraft whose pilots used slipping and skidding tricks to spoil the Japanese pilots' aim.

The Bell P-39 Airacobra could not turn as tightly as the Kittyhawk and the machines used at Moresby gave a lot of trouble with oil-leaking air-screws. The P-39's engine was more

vulnerable and there were many instances of landing gear trouble, but the plane was tough and as a ground-attack aircraft it fired devastating bursts with its 37mm cannon, two .50-inch and four .30-inch machine guns. Colonel Wagner, commander of the group of P-39 fighters, which were to relieve the Kittyhawks at the end of April, later reported: 'there has seldom been an even fight between Japanese Zero type fighters and our own. Only by virtue of armour-plate protection, leak-proof tanks, and ruggedness of construction of our fighter, have there not been a great many more of our pilots killed and airplanes destroyed. Our fighter pilots have

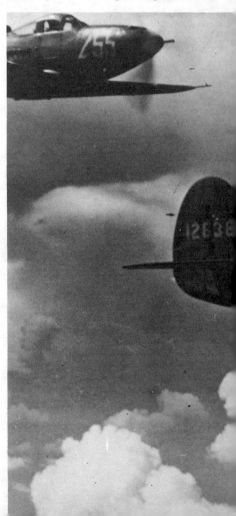

P-39 Airacobras suffered badly at the hands of the superior Zeros – and also from mechanical troubles

proven their courage and ability to fight continually against superior odds and still maintain a high morale. This high morale, however, has been with fighter pilots a forced one, with the knowledge that Japanese fighters would be just as high above tomorrow as they were today, and that the first encounter in combat would be an attack from out of the sun.'

On the day Sakai led his two wingmen into an attack from the sun on four P-39s, the ace shot down two with a couple of bursts while his fellow pilots claimed the other two. Sakai's account does not mention that day's action at Lae, recorded here from the RAAF official history documented from 75 Squadron records; but then there was so much action on either side of the high, jungle-clad mountains that Sakai confined his story to his own involvement. He mentions the fight over Moresby on 17th April, when thirteen Zeros escorted bombers bent on striking the spreading Allied base:

'With the bombers at 16,000 feet and my own group 1,500 feet higher, we crossed the Owen Stanley Range. Moresby slid into view. The seven Zeros closest to the bombers suddenly broke their protecting weaving and wheeled around in a tight climbing turn, still bunched together. P-40s, dropping from higher altitude to hit

the bombers, had been seen too soon, and the wedge of climbing Zeros split their ranks, spilling the fighters away from the lumbering heavyweights . . . Even as we rolled back into formation, the bombers and their fighter escorts were clawing in a maximum power climb . . . The bombers passed over Moresby and swung into their wide, slow turns, coming back this time for their bombing run, the sun now behind the pilots and the bombardiers. Hardly had the bombers slipped into their target runs when six fighters came at us from high altitude. I hauled back on the stick, standing the Zero on its tail. The other five fighters were glued to me as we turned directly into the enemy attack. We had no chance to fire; the enemy fighters rolled away and scattered, still diving. We returned to our escort weave positions. Miyazaki and his other two fighters had apparently gone crazy; they were swerving down, below the bombers . . . We passed Moresby and the bursting flak fell behind. I sighed with relief. Too soon! Nearly a mile above us, a single P-40 fighter dove with incredible speed. He came down so fast I could not move a muscle; one second he was above us, the next the lone plane plummeted like lightning into the bombers. Six hundred yards in front of me, I watched the fighter – he was going to ram! . . . How that plane ever got through the few yards' clearance between the third and fourth bombers of the left echelon, I shall never know. It seemed impossible, but it happened. With all guns blazing, the P-40 ripped through the bomber formation and poured a river of lead into Miyazaki's plane . . . Instantly the Zero burst into flames. With tremendous speed the P-40 disappeared far below.'

The fast-diving P-40 was Les Jackson, if the two records are exact. He wrote up his third kill in his log book that day; two others shared another Zero and Squadron Leader B B Cresswell, attached to 75 from 76 in training at Townsville, crashed into

a hill near Lae after an interception of his flight by enemy fighters. The final days of the squadron at Port Moresby are recorded in the RAAF Historical Section:

'Sergeant R J Granville was shot down in an interception over Moresby on 18th April. On the 21st eight Kittyhawks gave battle to eight enemy bombers escorted by Zeros. Flight Lieutenant A H Boyd and Pilot Officer Atherton shared a Zero, and four more were damaged. Three out of six P-40s were lost over Moresby on 24th April, when Pilot Officer O J Channon led a

52

formation of two. Pilot Officer Channon came down in flames near Porebada village and was killed. Sergeant M S Butler force-landed in a patch of grass at 200 miles an hour with undercarriage up. Flight Sergeant R W Crawford was forced down into the sea six miles west of Moresby after an enemy bullet had shot his throat microphone off and burned his neck. Both these were skilful forced landings and neither pilot was hurt.

'On the following day the unit moved to Eleven Mile Strip ... being hampered by a Zero strafing raid.

'Tragedy struck the squadron on 28th April, when the Commanding Officer, Squadron Leader John Jackson DFC, who had returned to his command only five days before, met his death.

'At about 10.30am on that sad day, eight enemy bombers and about fifteen Zeros came over. Five Kittyhawks, all that were serviceable, took off to meet the enemy. Jackson was leader and was accompanied by

P-40 in the striking Flying Tiger warpaint

Top : K143 Oscar. *Above :* Kittyhawk of 755 Squadron RAAF takes off
Below : Bristol Beaufort over New Britain after a bombing raid

Flying Officers Brereton, Cox and Masters and Sergeant Cowe.

'The Kittyhawks reached the bombers at 22,000 feet and could see five to seven Zeros swinging above them, with another two standing off. The Kittyhawks attacked the bombers from astern and the Zeros dived to engage them. Jackson was leading his flight in tight formation and he tried to avoid the leading Zero which had dived at him from above the bombers. His altitude was such that at his first attempt to manoeuvre he stalled and spun in attempting to avoid the Zero's attack. The other Kittyhawks also went into spins when attempting to avoid Jackson, but Brereton recovered and climbed again towards the bombers, opening fire at long range against a Zero. Brereton's aircraft was hit and he was badly injured. When Masters recovered from his spin he found himself some distance out to sea.

'Both Jackson and Cox were lost in this combat. But a Zero shot down but not claimed by any of the other three pilots must have been the victim of one or the other of the lost pilots. Jackson had been an inspiring and popular leader and was deeply mourned by his squadron. He was buried in a little cemetery overlooking the harbour at Moresby. His name was later given to one of the airstrips (Seven Mile) at Moresby.

'The following day his brother, Flight Lieutenant L D Jackson, took command of the squadron. On this day, too, eight bombers and Zeros raided the strip and three fighters came in low, strafing the runway and damaging one Kittyhawk.

'By the end of April 75 Squadron was nearly spent. Its hours for the month were 638, which included twelve on reconnaissance, 177 air fighting, 150 ferrying and 299 others. At the end of April it had three serviceable and seven unserviceable aircraft at Moresby. (Replacements had been sent up during the month.)

'On 30th April twenty-six Airacobras of the 35th and 36th American squadrons of the 8th Pursuit Group arrived at Moresby to take over the fighter defence of the area from the Kittyhawks. 75 Squadron had successfully held the fort until the arrival of this force and had borne the brunt of Japan's onslaught of Australia's last line of defence.

'The Airacobras began operations on 1st May, when they co-operated with the Kittyhawks on an interception. Sergeant D W Munro was shot down on the following day when three Kittyhawks and seven Airacobras intercepted a superior formation of enemy aircraft. Another aircraft was written off the same day when it crashed on take-off.

'No 75 Squadron made its last operational flight from Moresby on 3rd May 1942, when Pilot Officer A D Tucker, in the only remaining operationally serviceable Kittyhawk, joined eight Airacobras which intercepted twenty bombers and escorting Zeros. Tucker had to land with engine trouble, however, without coming into contact with the enemy.'

In forty-four days of combat duty as severe as any experienced by fighter pilots during the Battle of Britain, 75 Squadron had destroyed at least thirty-five, probably another fifteen, damaged about fifty for the loss of eleven pilots, including Cresswell, and the loss of twenty-two Kittyhawks, six of which were written off in accidents. In fighting incessantly until their aircraft were used up the Kittyhawk pilots may not have won an outright victory against the enemy but they saved Moresby from destruction, helped delay the movement aimed at the port's capture, and gave the Allied air forces time to form more squadrons on the training grounds. Les Jackson took his squadron back to the comforts of the south for a long rest before they re-equipped with new P-40s and trained replacement pilots in readiness for their next New Guinea assignment which was to help win a land battle.

Milne Bay

While the Australians' first Kitty-hawk squadron in the SWPA was battling with the enemy in New Guinea, two other squadrons, 76 and 77, were forming with pilots from the European and Middle East fighting, and from Operational Training Units. Some of the experienced men had fought against a wide range of German, Italian and Vichy French aircraft and the newly appointed leader of 76 Squadron, Squadron Leader Peter Turnbull, a former flight commander from 75 Squadron, was a veteran P-40 pilot from the Desert War. The squadron was to help in the winning of the forthcoming land battle. 77 Squadron was also formed at this time in Western Australia from where it flew to Darwin defence operations. One of its pilots ran out of petrol during an exercise off the coast and made a forced landing on Melville Island. He was Pilot Officer J G Gorton, at the time of writing Prime Minister of Australia. This squadron too was eventually based at Milne Bay but by then the land battle was over.

Other experienced men in 76 Squadron had won their spurs in Spitfires over England and France. Truscott, Wawn, Tainton and Elphick had flown together in 452 Squadron, RAAF, a Spitfire squadron which began operations across the Channel in July 1941, instructed, encouraged and often led by the legendary ace 'Paddy' Finucane DSO, DFC and two bars, who had shot down over twenty aircraft by the time he was twenty-one. An Australian RAF Squadron Leader, R W Bungey, was the CO and Finucane a flight commander until he left 452 to command an RAF squadron. The young Irishman had shown the Australians all the tricks of the trade in fighting Me 109s and FW 190s, and 'Bluey' (for his red hair) Truscott was his star pupil. In January 1942 Bungey was given a fighter station to command

and Truscott was promoted to the operational command. He had been a star Australian Rules footballer in Melbourne before joining the Air Force, one of the aggressive, rugged, forthright athletic types who stood out as potential leaders in the air. Keith Truscott's first major mission as CO was to lead his Spitfires out over the Channel when the *Gneisenau, Scharnhorst* and *Prinz Eugen* escaped from Brest under the cover of German fighters and low clouds that formed a heavy overcast in the winter skies. The Royal Navy had only a few destroyers and MTBs stationed anywhere near the German warships. 452 joined two other Spitfire squadrons to form a wing, led by Finucane, to fly through the murk and over the ships but they were unable to find the air fighting. The squadrons then separated to seek targets for themselves, Truscott leading his down to the sea where through the mist he saw what he believed to be an enemy transport. He committed his twelve Spitfires to a fast beam-on attack before he realised that he was attacking a large destroyer thickly spiked with flak guns. The surprise and shock did not alter the course of the Spitfires. They flew into a wall of bursting flak, following their leader and firing cannon and machine guns across the ship until it was silenced. The Spitfires returned intact except for a few shrapnel and bullet holes and the plastic hood shot away from the leader's cockpit.

When the veterans of the Desert and European air war had returned to lend their experience to RAAF squadrons in their homeland, they found there were not enough formations to give to former commanders; some were demoted and others managed to hold their rank. When 76 Squadron flew in to Milne Bay three of its pilots held the rank of Squadron Leader. The squadron was the first to land at Milne Bay, followed by the rested and re-equipped 75 Squadron, still led by Les Jackson. Turnbull's P-40s were somewhat worn from weeks of intense training and Jackson's were brand new; within six weeks they would all be severely worn, not from air fighting but from continuous use in ground support, for they were to become aerial artillery supporting infantry during the battle which would end with Japan's first defeat on land in the Pacific war.

The inexorable determination of Yamamoto and the Japanese High Command to continue with their plan to capture Port Moresby, after the Coral Sea battle and the disastrous losses at Midway, can only be compared with Hitler's orders which sent legions to their death on the Russian front. Yamamoto knew that Moresby was a rapidly expanding base which the Allies would defend with all their resources; he gambled that the slowness of the Allies in increasing the number of their battalions would give him time, and a reasonable chance of success, to attack from the north of Papua over the Owen Stanley Range. On 18th July the orders were issued: elements of General Hyakutake's Seventeenth Army were to land at Buna for the overland move and the navy's *Kawaguchi* Force was to land at Milne Bay, which would be useful as a strategic naval and air base east of Moresby. This move was to be followed by the capture of Samarai Island in a staged movement along the coast to the ultimate goal. On paper, these moves appeared to be reasonable. In practice they were a fatal error.

General MacArthur had chosen the Buna Bay site as his first forward base, a choice also made by the enemy who got there first, landing during the night of 21st July with two more troop-laden convoys following by the end of the month. Mitchells, Marauders, B17s and Dauntless dive-bombers attacked the convoys coming in and going out, ineffectually except for a couple of direct hits: the bombers and Airacobras caused real damage on the beachhead, hitting troop positions and supply dumps. Five of seven Daunt-

lesses which struck at the last convoy were shot down by Zeros. The Buna landings were part of a larger Japanese operation which would extend northwest along 140 miles of coast to Lae.

The landing at Buna was made against light opposition from a small force of Australians, the New Guinea Volunteers, the 2/5th Independent Company, a platoon of infantry and a mortar platoon. Collectively known as Kanga Force, they had skilfully operated around Lae during June, mapping Japanese positions and destroying trucks, buildings, bridges and isolating groups of enemy troops, using sub-machine guns, mortars, sticky-bombs and packets of TNT. Hyakutake's 13,500-strong division pushed forward from Buna and Gona through the jungle-clad hills and high mountains along the Kokoda Trail, much of which was a mere native path winding upwards beneath the thick forests. At Kokoda, on the northern foothills about forty miles inland by air, was a small airfield, the first objective in the enemy's drive. Reinforced by Militia, Kanga Force skirmished in guerrilla fashion as it retreated back to Kokoda, existing on the army's canned beef and hard biscuits dropped to them by 'biscuit bomber' supply aircraft.

The Australians were to retreat to within fifty miles of Port Moresby before a battle-hardened brigade of the AIF 7th Division, recently returned from the Middle East, arrived in Port Moresby to begin their climb up the southern side of the Kokoda Trail and lend their weight to the exhausted Kanga Force. From where the short road ended at Uberi, not far from the base, the track rose 1,200 feet in the first three miles, much of it negotiated by the 'golden stairs' – log steps held by stakes and behind each log a puddle of mud. The men of the 7th were quite confident that they, if anybody, could

The Lae field, 7th August 1942. Bombs burst on runway from attack delivered at 3,400 feet

stop the 'invincible' Japanese. Fortunately, they were to have reasonable air support. Since the days when 75 Squadron saved Moresby from obliteration, the Allies possessed a stronger fighter force and their bombers, army co-operation and transport plane numbers were increasing. By the end of July, Japanese army groups moving over the mountains had reached Kokoda and taken the small airfield; there were more Japanese moving up than there were Australian soldiers between Kokoda and Moresby. With the fall of Buna, MacArthur sought to lay blame on the Allied bombers for not sinking the transports and replaced Brett with Major-General George C Kenney to command the Allied Air Forces, SWPA.

With the movement of Japanese ground forces over the Owen Stanley Range, the possibility of a Japanese occupation of Milne Bay on the distant eastern flank of Papua was confirmed by Intelligence. So an army group,

Milne Force, under the command of Major-General C A Clowes CBE, DSO, MC, was sent to garrison the bay and the settlement of Gili Gili plantation. Milne Force consisted of two infantry brigades – 18th Brigade from the AIF 7th Division and 7th Militia Brigade, totalling some 4,500 infantrymen, service troops and over 1,300 American engineers. Number One Strip, called Gurney, constructed inland from the centre of the bay by the engineers, was virtually a swamp laid with a matting of interlocked perforated steel plates, forming a runway 5,000 feet long by 80 feet wide. A second strip was planned while preparatory clearing for a third, a few miles north east along the coast, had begun, forming a long avenue between the coconut palms. Gurney Strip was about two miles and the third strip about a mile from the sea, and the centre of Gili Gili was in between the two strips which were five miles apart. The rainy season had begun and during the forth-

Left : 75 Squadron pilots, Port Moresby ; Squadron Leader L D Jackson second from left. *Above :* US Lieutenant-General George C Kenny

coming battle heavy rain was to fall for ninety per cent of the time, nonstop for hours on end, the clouds coming down to about 1,000 feet and the hot, steaming earth generating mists to add to the murk. The torrential downpour covered Gurney with so much water that waves rose in front of the landing Kittyhawks. Soon the frequent landings and take-offs turned the surface into a muddy slush.

On the way over from Australia 76 Squadron staged at Port Moresby where Turnbull decided to try out improvised bomb racks which had been fitted to some of the Kittyhawks. He and Flight Lieutenant Sullivan led two flights with a group of escorting P-39s to bomb anti-aircraft positions at Napapo and landing barges on the beach at Gona, and then proceed to Gurney Strip at Milne Bay. The escort was lost near the target, Sullivan's flight bombed but failed to observe the results and Turnbull's flight had to

jettison their loads when attacked by enemy fighters, after which they flew on to Gurney. Sullivan's flight returned to Moresby without the leader who later walked in, having force-landed a few miles away on the coast. The operation was the first Kittyhawk dive-bombing raid in the South West Pacific Area.

The total Japanese invasion force was fewer than the defenders'; originally intended for Milne Bay, the 124th Regiment had been hurriedly diverted to Guadalcanal where American Marines had landed to prevent an enemy occupation, setting the stage for another grim campaign. Two forces were sent out against Milne Bay. A small group of about 350 men moved down in barges from Buna to make a planned flank approach overland from the northern Papuan village of Taupota on the Goodenough Bay coast, and the major group which was made up of the 3rd *Kure* Naval Landing Force, the 5th *Kure* Naval Landing Force, the 10th Naval Labour Corps and the 5th *Sasebo* Naval Landing Force left Rabaul in two transports, escorted by two cruisers, three destroyers and two submarine chasers, to land at the heart of the bay close to the strips. The Japanese order for the operation briefly described the tactics and defined the objective: 'At the dead of night quickly complete the landing and strike the white soldiers without reserve. Unitedly smash to pieces the enemy lines and take the aerodrome by storm.'

There was a radar unit at Milne Bay as well as a signals station which remained silent, as did the radios of the P-40s until the Japanese could discover by other means what aircraft and troops were stationed there. The Japanese saw for themselves on 4th August when four Zeros and a dive-bomber ran into a patrol of five Kittyhawks over the new base. They may have been lost, for one had its undercarriage down for a landing; if so they certainly realised their mistake in thinking that they were over one of

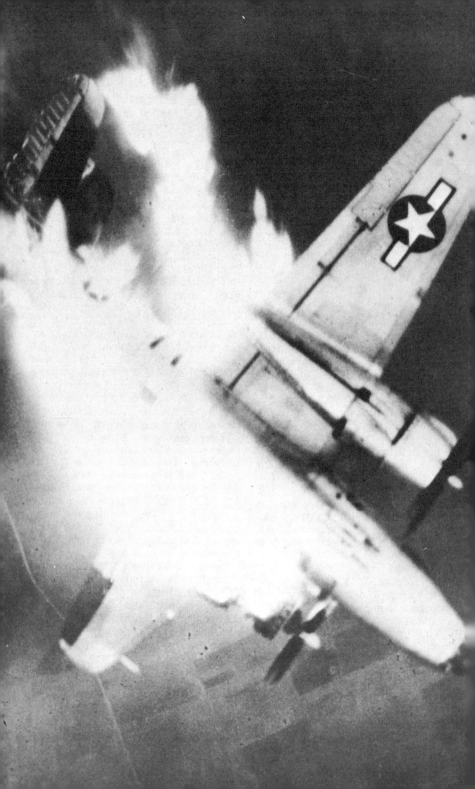

their own fields when the Kittyhawks attacked, shooting down the dive-bomber. The Zeros escaped after destroying one of 75 Squadron's Kittyhawks on the ground but were caught on their flight north and one was shot down by Flying Officer Max Bott and Sergeant P Dempster. On the 7th, Kittyhawks flew too far on an interception attempt and five force-landed, one crashing on the emergency strip at Goodenough Island. A second interception of twelve Japanese fighters was made four days later. Although outnumbered by the twenty-two P-40s sent up, the Japanese shot down four Australians for a loss of four of their own. There was a respite from air attack over the next fortnight during which time the AIF brigade arrived to prepare their defence positions; at the end of this period the enemy transports arrived.

Landing a fighter on Gurney Strip was a rare experience. At first the pilots found it difficult to control their planes, skidding and sometimes swinging off the matting to bog in the soft mud, where ground staff sweated in the slush to manhandle the heavy fighters to matting-floored dispersal bays among the coconut plantations. The steaming humid atmosphere, the high incidence of malaria and the appalling living conditions were enough to try the spirit of both pilots and ground crews. And there was the added threat of being cut off from outside help; they were all more or less in the front line and were prepared to fight it out to the end.

Constant watch on the now large enemy base at Rabaul provided Allied Intelligence with information from which most of the enemy's major moves could be predicted, and projected landings at Guadalcanal, Milne Bay and Port Moresby were forecast at GHQ. As the photographed transports and warships showed by mid-August that they were about to move,

Martin Marauder blazes earthwards after a fatal encounter

the necessity for armed reconnaissance from Milne Bay was imperative. A Hudson bomber squadron, 6 RAAF, was moved up in haste from New South Wales and all the P-40s were modified to carry bombs. The Hudsons were based at Horn Island, at the tip of Queensland's Cape York Peninsula and staged through Port Moresby or Milne Bay on their missions. One flight was stationed at Milne Bay.

The action began on the 24th. A Coastwatcher on Cape Nelson observed seven enemy barges, fifty feet long and ten feet wide, moving down along the coast. It was expected that they would carry troops and supplies to a point on this northern part of the coast, for a flanking movement, rather than travel right up to the bay's entrance and then another twenty miles up the bay to Gili Gili. At the same time as the barge sighting was received at Milne Bay, several Zeros had attacked the strip in what proved to be a futile attempt to strafe aircraft, most of which were parked behind barricades of coconut logs. The slit trenches were always full of water, anyone jumping to safety was drenched, and usually the aircraftsmen, from cooks to fitters, fired at strafers with machine guns, rifles and pistols. In this raid a crash-landed US Liberator was destroyed but it had already been written off. Patrolling Kittyhawks caught the Zeros as they came out of low cloud cover, two were shot down, two were probables and others were hit and damaged without any P-40 loss. There was plenty of time for hunting the slow moving barges.

The main Japanese force was reported that day to be near Normanby Island, steaming straight for the wide entrance to Milne Bay. The base was alerted and an Allied destroyer was ordered to leave the bay to avoid certain destruction. The hospital ship *Manunda*, repaired after the bombing at Darwin, accepted the risk of being attacked again despite its Red Cross markings, and stayed. General Clowes assumed command of all Allied land and air forces at the base. Without reserves or much hope of receiving any, without tanks, coastal guns or searchlights, the soldiers and airmen tensely waited for the enemy to make his expected night landings.

The Kittyhawks were held back until midday on the 25th – until a report of the whereabouts of the Buna barges had been received. Then it was found that the barges were lying against the shore of the western coast of Goodenough Island. Two flights, one acting as top cover, were sent out to destroy them. In run after run the P-40s strafed until every barge was set alight from the firing of 10,000 rounds of ammunition. Some enemy troops were killed on the beach and on the barges but most of them had gone on to the island where they were left stranded and out of the coming battle.

Attention was then centred on the main convoy, approaching at a rate which should bring it through the entrance at midnight. Allied Air Headquarters ordered a B-17 bomber raid on the ships which remained hidden under the thick cloud cover and were not found by the high-flying Fortresses. Early in the afternoon a flight of Les Jackson's squadron took off, each plane carrying a 300-lb bomb, escorting a flight of Hudsons on an attack on the convoy. The only success was a near-miss by a bomb from one of the Hudsons which slowed down a submarine chaser. A couple of hours later nine P-40s took off with bombs. For the second time in the war Truscott led a formation of fighters low across the water into the mouths of naval anti-aircraft guns, this time concentrating on transports loaded with troops, the most important targets, and he continued to attack until every round was spent. With the cloud base too low for dive-bombing, the P-40s were tested in low-level bombing for the first time and they missed. Turnbull's fighter-bomber P-40s also missed in their low-

level drop and his flight too used up their ammunition in strafing the transports. The Hudsons made a mast-top run and stopped a destroyer. No airmen were hit and the P-40s were unscathed except for one ditched near the entrance to the bay, the pilot later being rescued from a small island. Flying from Moresby, medium bombers and P-39s lent their support by pounding Lae and Buna, and searching for enemy shipping along the coast.

The raining, misty murk of evening was closing in as the Kittyhawks rearmed, refuelled and took off again but could not find the convoy in the darkness. It was difficult enough to find the strip again and to land beside the flare-path, skidding and spraying through the squelching muck. Two Hudsons took off to make another low-level attack at dusk, to be hit by intense anti-aircraft fire as they scored another near-miss. In pitch blackness at midnight the transports moved up into the bay, observed by the crew of a RAAF crash launch. At 0130hrs the enemy troops disembarked into barges for the run in to the beach.

That night, the fighter pilots helped the ground crews servicing and arming the Kittyhawks for the coming battle, while sounds of sporadic fighting came from the shore. The night hid the enemy who might be landing in hundreds or in thousands. No one at Milne Bay had ever heard of any Japanese invasion being repulsed, yet the men of AIF were confident that with the RAAF pilots covering them, they could handle any number of Japs; and the pilots were just as confident in the 'Diggers'. The Militia troops had yet to prove themselves in battle. Clowes had placed them in what he expected to be the front line, keeping his veterans in reserve a few miles inland. The line was manned in company strength at various points from near the end of the bay back along the northern side to a distance of five or six miles. Clowes gambled that they would land on this side, the

Top: Boston roars over downed and wrecked Japanese planes at Lae
Above: RAAF Hudson over Timor. *Below:* Australians advance warily through jungle at Buna

closest to Taupota where the barge-borne Japanese were to have landed. The enemy's first objective was the little earth road, now soaked and boggy, which ran along the narrow coastal strip and the foothills of the mountains, the area thick with jungle and nowhere more than a mile wide, and at one place the mountains squeezed it down to a matter of yards. The ground was soft with rain and seepage, and secondary growth covered the track. Here, between KB Mission and Anthioma, the powerful steel barges landed the enemy who quickly moved onto the track which led to Rabi and thence by a slightly better road to Gili Gili and Gurney Strip. As long as they concentrated on that side, Clowes could use his forces to the best advantage.

Before dawn, B Company of the 61st Battalion was in action at the Mission and Kittyhawk pilots sat in their fighters waiting for enough light to enable them to take off and find targets along the beach; the transports and warships, for all their shell-firing, were not as important now as the enemy attacking from the beach. An AIF liaison officer, Captain Thompson, worked closely with the RAAF at their Operations tent, informing the airmen of the ground situation and the army's needs and advising the army on how and where the planes could strike.

The first and obvious need was to hit the barges and troops on the beach. The false dawn light was dimmed by low clouds as the Kittyhawks and Hudsons took off for the

six-mile flight across the plantation to the bay and the barges at the edge of the shore. All the barges in sight were hit, some were sunk, the others protected by their steel structure but nevertheless damaged, an ammunition-laden truck was repeatedly attacked until it exploded, drums of fuel being floated across to the beach were set alight and, where the army indicated troops in the jungle, the trees and bushes were strafed with thousands of rounds of ammunition. Probably the simplest, or easiest action to accomplish – the sinking of barges – was the most strategically damaging to the Japanese: their barge losses at Goodenough Island cancelled a flank attack from Taupota and those lost near the Mission in the first few hours

of the battle spoiled ship-to-shore ferrying facilities and the possible use of barge-manoeuvring along the coast to by-pass and surround pockets of defence, tactics used so successfully by the Japanese in Malaya.

Number 75 pilots vowed never to shave one side of their faces, number 76 never to shave theirs on the opposite side, until the Japanese were driven into the sea. Half shaven, they flew sorties all day, strafing and bombing, landing and taking off time after time from the frightful strip.

The Japanese were equipped with rifles, machine guns, mortars and light tanks fitted with tracks spanning ten feet. The soldiers advanced, laughing and singing nervously as they moved into a morass of flowing mud and tangled wilderness. Having discharged its troops, the convoy retreated from the scene and was at last discovered by searching B-17s. The bombers had better luck this time, damaging a cruiser and, more severely, one of the transports. One Fortress exploded in the air. What was needed were specialists, Nimitz's dive-bombers and torpedo-planes, to attack through the rain and sink the warships and transports, but they were busy elsewhere. B-26 Marauders sought the convoy and were intercepted by a flight of Zeros, one of which was shot down and ditched in the sea. As it was close to the shore and might be salvaged by the Allies, two other Zeros dived down to destroy it, regardless of their fellow pilot still clinging to a wing. Jackson and Flight Sergeant Riddel happened to fly onto the scene as the Zeros were making their attack and shot them both down. The pilot in the water survived the Marauder and Zero attacks and was taken prisoner.

Eight Val dive-bombers and a dozen Zeros made the expected raid on the strip on the morning of the 27th. Radar picked up their approach and 75

RAAF Kittyhawk lands at Milne Bay. Vigilant Bofors crew in foreground

Squadron fighters were ready for them, shooting down five bombers and two Zeros for the loss of one Kittyhawk pilot. Late in the afternoon 76 Squadron lost its commander. Searching for light tanks, Turnbull and his wingman spotted a group of enemy soldiers near the Mission and dived to strafe. Suddenly Turnbull's plane flicked over and dived into the ground: he could have been hit by ground fire or an accumulation of mud might have affected the aircraft's flying qualities and caused a high-speed stall. The loss of the popular and experienced leader was a severe blow to the airmen at Milne Bay. Because he had won a bulldogging competition before the war he was sometimes called the 'Flying Cowboy', or 'Tomahawk Pete' from his experiences in P-40s during the Western Desert battles. When the third strip at Milne Bay was completed it was named Turnbull Strip. His place at the head of 76 Squadron was taken by Keith Truscott.

All day on the 27th the fighters maintained strafing attacks, many of the sorties made blind against the jungle covering, others made with successful strikes observed. At dusk the Japanese troops made their attack against the Mission, portable searchlights blazing through the rain to show the way and to blind the defenders who had only rifle and machine gun defence against the armoured tanks. Enemy destroyers raced up the bay to add the weight of their shellfire in this major attack which gave the Japanese the Mission and use of the cleared road to the third strip. By dawn they had reached it and were only two miles from where the Kittyhawks operated. The P-40s' guns were now firing almost as soon as their wheels were retracted.

The few Hudsons also sortied as often as refuelling and rearming could be effected in the mud and rain that drenched the men rolling bombs and drums of fuel up to the bombers. B-26

Flying Fortress MkIIA rises from
coastal airstrip at start of bombing
mission

Battalion until this second morning
when the AIF 2/10th Battalion was
brought up to assist them. Although
the Japanese had their few tanks, and
the Australians were without anti-
tank guns, the struggle was between
opposing infantry. During daylight,
the enemy sent snipers into the tops of
palm trees, a favourite Japanese
tactic, and the P-40s were sent to strafe
in front of the lines which were so
close that sometimes Australian
soldiers were in the line of aircraft
fire. Knocking down invisible snipers
from trees could only be effected by
raking the complete foliage with a
concentration of fire. This produced
results: 'palm fronds, bullets and dead
Japanese were pouring down with the
rain,' reported one army observer. In
the early hours of the 28th, Truscott
led a flight of four machines in close
co-operation with the army against
troop positions which were being
established at the far end of the third
strip. Attacking what appeared to be
a headquarters, the P-40s made half a
dozen runs over the exposed enemy,
killing over fifty of them. Visibility
through the rain and low misty cloud
was reduced to a few hundred yards.
Gurney Strip was a quagmire of oozing
mud and with so much manhandling
of fuel drums and bogged-down planes
during servicing and re-arming, the
fitters had to be helped by other ground
staff.

Marauders from Port Moresby came
up to add their weight, led down
through the heavy rain by Kittyhawk
pilots who now had an intimate
knowledge of the front line area and
its targets. Gurney Strip was no place
for pilots not used to landing in a sea
of mud – Marauders and other bombers
could best assist by flying over from
Moresby. In any case it was now a job
for local close-contact fighters. Bombers could only really be effectively
used if the enemy brought up more
transports laden with reinforcements.
The small garrison felt that there
were enough Japanese about already.
To hold the tanks, Clowes brought up
his few 25-pounder guns closer to the
front line.

Had the Japanese landed at Gili
Gili itself they could reasonably have
taken Gurney Strip and, with their
fighters in possession, won the battle.
As it was they now made the third
strip an objective. General Clowes left
the brunt of the fighting to the 61st

During that day air attacks continued and thousands of rounds were
fired into the trees. On the beaches
stores were destroyed and in the bay
barges were set alight when incendiary
bullets hit their power units. P-40s
escorted Marauders until they dropped
their bombs and then went down to
strafe on their own. The Japanese had
gained a stronger foothold at the end
of the third strip, which could give
them a long scrub-free approach for
tanks and infantry in a swift night

attack towards the centre of the air force camp and on to Gurney strip. Believing that there was a danger to the fighters on the ground, HQ at Moresby that evening ordered the planes back there. If the fighters were destroyed on the strip the extra arm of the army would be lost, some of the pressure would be lifted from the enemy and he would be in a safer position to bring up seaborne reinforcements. Their departure was a disappointment to the troops who were not aware of the plans, and Truscott was completely against the move; he stayed behind with the ground crews, also disappointed but consoled at least with the knowledge that a thorough maintenance at Moresby would freshen the P-40s. The following day a Hudson navigated for the returning fighters. There had been trouble on the way to Moresby. One pilot was killed in a crash, and, on the way back, Jackson was forced down along the coast from where he returned

after a three-day journey by native canoe – manned by twenty Papuan women – and lugger.

On the fifth day of the attack the Japanese spared Gurney Strip in what developed into nightly naval shelling, for they planned to use it themselves, if their marines could capture it. During the night, Japanese naval units fired shells into the Milne Bay area but they fell wide of the target and mainly in the hills. This shelling tactic became a regular feature of the night fighting which was more intense than during the day, when they concentrated on sniping. On one occasion an RAAF crash-launch was caught in the beam of a searchlight and sunk by shellfire, three men being killed; two escaped overboard, one drifting across the bay for eighteen hours until he neared an enemy-held shore where he was helped by natives who hid him under an upturned canoe. A Hudson reconnoitreing the sea approaches that afternoon had sighted a cruiser and eight destroyers, an ominous collection that could be bringing reinforcements. The Hudson attacked under the low cloud to score possible damage on a destroyer with a near-miss. Also, that afternoon, a light mountain gun, which had been giving the army so much trouble, was put out of action in an attack by Truscott and his wingman. Kittyhawks were sent out to attack the warships again hidden by the screen of cloud and rain so the pilots delivered their bomb-loads to the enemy on land. Another P-40 skidded wildly on landing along the slush and the pilot was killed when the plane crashed into the trees.

'Old John' Jackson had once refused when requested by HQ to move his planes from Moresby when ten had been lost in the first few days. Now

Left: Beaufighter of 30 Squadron over Papua. *Below:* Truscott taxis to dispersal area at Milne Bay after an operation

Truscott refused to permit his squadron to fly back to the safe base, even for one night. He insisted that they stay, not only for the fight but for the morale of the troops which could be affected, under the prevailing conditions, if they found their air support had been withdrawn. A strong bond had been established between the pilots and the infantry.

Infiltration by the enemy was constantly expected at the air force camp which had its own patrols and a barrier of mine-fields laid by the American engineers. On the 29th, disaster struck. A herd of zebu cattle wandered into a heavily mined clearing; a couple were killed in explosions and a fusillade was fired to chase the cattle away. The canteen with its small stock of beer and cigarettes had been mined for destruction should it happen to fall to the enemy, and now it went up. Some quick-acting airman had heard the explosions and by firing at the minefield had made sure there would

be no canteen left for the enemy.

That evening the RAAF kept its fighters at Milne Bay, 1,000 yards from the front line, determined to keep them in readiness to assist the army whenever and wherever it was possible to bomb and strafe the enemy. The ground position was static for the following two days, the battle in the balance while the Militia and the 2/10th Battalion held the Japanese. When they made a strong attack to move up the third strip on the 31st, the 2/9th and 2/12th Battalions, Clowes' strong but final reserves, went into action, inflicting heavy losses and driving the Japanese back. The warships were sighted again on 2nd September by a Hudson flying through foul weather and semi-darkness, too late however to bring out the rest of the small air force. That night, and for the next two nights, naval bombardment concentrated on the Australian defences with little physical effect although causing tension and expectancy of a further landing in force. Nevertheless, throughout the base an air of confidence was beginning to prevail among army and air force men. The shattered stump of a coconut palm at the end of the third strip marked the westernmost point of the Japanese advance and where nearly a hundred Japanese marines had been bulldozed into a common grave. The 'invincible' Japanese had been held.

Clowes planned his counterattack for the night of the 5th September, at the end of an afternoon when Kittyhawks bombed and strafed while the artillery laid down a heavy barrage and mortars lobbed bombs along the coastal track, from the plantation to the Mission. As the troops advanced and fought in the dark they could hear the movement of ship-to-shore barge activity. The following morning, instead of finding a strongly reinforced enemy, opposition was lighter as the

AIF men advanced up to what had been the main Japanese camp, abandoned and littered with supplies.

Truscott and Jackson continued to lead their squadrons on numerous sorties against ground targets, mostly hidden and obscure, sprayed anyway with machine gun fire. Replacing machine gun barrels was part of daily maintenance routine. So many rounds and so much mud getting into the barrels wore away the rifling, the .50-inch bore enlarging to .60-inch. Bullets scattered widely around targets when the barrels became so badly worn. Ammunition was always available – supplies had been brought in by the motor vessel *Anshun* – and in emergency more could have been flown in from Moresby. The supply vessel was not sunk at the Gili Gili wharf until the night of the 6th, during a searchlight and shelling display. The illuminated *Manunda* was also picked up by the Japanese searchlights but was not fired on.

The large enemy base at Rabaul, which General Arnold described as a 'Pearl Harbor in reverse', was kept under observation and often bombed during these desperate days of battle at Milne Bay. These, and raids on other Japanese air bases, accounted for the lack of counter air-hammering by Vals, Bettys and Zeros. With the tide of battle turned, the obvious place now for Allied attack aircraft was Gurney Strip, but it was not until the American engineers designed a kind of bulldozer-squeegee to sweep away the liquid mud that the strip was safe for strangers. Once this was done the air force sent up some Beaufort bombers which could also carry torpedoes, and three Beaufighters-long-range cannon-firing two-place fighters with twin radial engines so quiet that they were, it is said, called 'Whispering Death' by the Japanese. The reliable Hudson scouts found, on the 7th, a target for the newcomers. An attack by three Hudsons, sixteen Kittyhawks, two Beaufighters and six Beauforts was mounted against a

This shot of Martin B-26 Marauders in formation clearly shows the aircraft's armament and fine lines

Tired but determined Australians advance through swamp on the way to Buna

cruiser and a destroyer near Normanby Island. Yet again the Japanese escaped with only 'severe damage' claimed by the attackers. At least there was some consolation: by not checking this move into Milne Bay the air force saved the army some work, for the two ships came up that night to evacuate most of the remnants of the defeated Japanese ground forces. The ships also shelled the base and again played their searchlights on the *Manunda*, which was spared.

The army had committed its reserves at the right moment and the battle was over. General MacArthur had been very apprehensive about the outcome of the two-week battle and sourly commented: 'The enemy's defeat at Milne Bay must not be accepted as a measure of the relative fighting capacity of the troops involved.' Field-Marshal Sir William Slim, who was at that time commanding Allied forces which were suffering defeats in Burma, later wrote in his memoirs regarding Milne Bay: 'It was Australian soldiers who first broke the spell of the invincibility of the Japanese army.' In his report to General Blamey, General Clowes stated: 'the action of 75 and 76 Squadrons RAAF on the first day was probably the decisive factor . . . incessant attacks over three days proved the decisive factor in the enemy's decision to re-embark what was left of his forces.' Another factor was that, for the first time, it was the Allies and not the Japanese who controlled the skies.

About 300 Kittyhawk gun barrels were pitted, rusted and worn out from firing 200,000 rounds of ammunition, even though on many occasions there were gun stoppages. Mud and water damaged flaps which had to be replaced and the numerous landings on steel matting had worn smooth the tread on the tyres. The work performed by the maintenance staff and their non-technical helpers was remarkable considering the conditions under which they slaved, drenched and muddied and lacking the cover and normal facilities of workshop or hangar, and with malaria prevalent among them. Although there were very few awards handed out to the pilots, they were pleased to learn later that their cooks received a clasp for their successful efforts to tastefully camouflage the bully beef and biscuits. Truscott received no official recognition at the time but, like the cooks, was awarded a Mention in Despatches about a year later. By then he was dead. The pilot for whom the 'Redheads of Britain' contributed to buy a Spitfire was killed when his Kittyhawk dived into the sea after making a dummy attack too low, on a Catalina he had been escorting. After Milne Bay, his squadron had rested and later moved to the North-Western area where he shot down a bomber in a moonlight interception, and had once again flown a Spitfire borrowed from his old squadron which had come out from England to help defend Darwin.

Right: Replacements for a late production P-40N of 76 Squadron
Below: Preparing to leave for a mission over Dutch New Guinea

76

Snarling shark mouths add a fearsome touch to this Lockheed C-38B Lightning

At the end of September the Kitty-hawks left Milne Bay, relieved by P-39 squadrons of the USAAF. It was unlikely that the Japanese would make a second attempt to land troops there. They were fully occupied in the Solomons where US Marines were also breaking the spell of Japanese invincibility. Regardless of their failure to reach Port Moresby via Milne Bay or after the Coral Sea battle, the Japanese High Command insisted on forcing through the Kokoda Trail in an effort to reach the port. Early in September at least 1,000 fresh troops were landed in Papua to reinforce the 4,000 already facing the Australians in the Owen Stanley Range. An epic fight in appalling conditions across the rainy, precipitous, jungle-clad mountains, a two-month series of skirmishes and hand-to-hand combat, resulted in the defeat of General Horii's brigades and withdrawal to the large garrisons at Buna, Gona, Lae and Salamaua. By the end of October 1942, Port Moresby was secure.

Although the importance of the role fighters would play in a modern war was not fully appreciated by senior commanders of the Allied services in the late 1930s, the few influential enthusiasts struggled hard enough against a general apathy to develop hard-hitting interceptors and the P-40 emerged in time. The myth of the impregnability of turret-armed bombers was soon exploded when the fighting began. The only time when the various types of bombers could wreak their havoc was when their escort fighter force was strong enough to clear the skies. Until then, even fighter-bombers – such as the vaunted Bf 110 'Destroyer' – were vulnerable.

Undoubtedly the P-40 was the most important aircraft in the Pacific land areas during the most vital and desperate period of the war against Japan. By the time they had fulfilled their purpose in denying the enemy his chances to dominate the skies over Darwin and Port Moresby, and had so remarkably contributed to the victory at Milne Bay, other aircraft, notably Beaufighters, P-38 Lightnings and B-25 Mitchell bombers, were ready to take the war to the enemy's extensive

South Pacific possessions. General Kenney's Allied Air Force offensive in 1943 returned tenfold the bombing and strafing delivered by the Japanese air forces, and Allied army divisions advanced over the Papuan mountains of New Guinea and invaded islands, retaking bases which were to become stepping-stones on the way to Japan itself.

The effect of superior Allied air power early in 1943 was dramatically illustrated on 3rd March. The Japanese hold on the northern coast of New Guinea, where bases were established from Buna to Lae, was threatened by advancing Australian and newly arrived American army divisions. With his fighter cover resources dissipated in carrier battles and earlier Papuan and Solomon Islands actions, Yamamoto risked sending reinforcements by sea to Lae, without a large umbrella of Zeros. Although P-40s were not involved in what became known as the Battle of the Bismarck Sea, it was partly because of the fighters' use at Port Moresby and Milne Bay that Allied land-planes were ready to attack the Japanese convoy and inflict the greatest blow the enemy had suffered during these campaigns.

A watch kept on shipping movement at Rabaul and knowledge of the Japanese navy's signal code enabled Allied Intelligence to predict the size of the convoy and the direction it would take, so that all the Allied Air Force attack units in New Guinea were given ample time to co-ordinate their strikes. Plans were drawn up which provided for either a split convoy or the entire group to be hit as they approached the area where range would be suitable for all types of planes Apart from reconnaissance and escort aircraft, the size of the force readied for action was thirty-seven heavy bombers, forty-nine medium and light bombers and ninety-six fighters; there were Fortresses, Liberators, Mitchells, Douglas Bostons (Havocs), Beaufighters and Lightnings. Thick tropical storm clouds covered the sealanes until 1st March when a reconnoitering Liberator sighted through the breaking weather eight transports escorted by eight destroyers; they were some forty miles from the coast, heading west, and were escorted by Zeros.

Pilots often added a personal touch to their machines. 'U-Bute', and in the background, 'Peter's Revenge'

RAAF Bostons at dawn the following morning bombed and strafed the Lae airfield to neutralise the enemy fighters there. When the convoy was next found a group of Fortresses made the first attack, mortally damaging a transport which stayed afloat long enough to transfer its troops to a destroyer. Three Zeros were shot down during this and a later attack by Fortresses that day.

During the night the convoy was shadowed by Catalinas and on the following morning, when the ships were about thirty miles south-east of Finschhafen, they were within striking range of all the other aircraft. High-flying Lightnings over Fortresses and Beaufighters formating with Mitchells assembled after take-off from the Moresby strips, and Bostons again went over the range to harass the Lae Wing. About eighty planes made the assault on the convoy that morning. Lightnings dived on the Zeros as they made for the Fortresses which opened the attack, gunners and Lightning pilots shooting down twenty enemy fighters for the loss of three Lightnings and a Fortress;

the Fortress crew bailed out but, hanging in parachutes, were machine gunned by Zeros. A ship was sunk and fires started on another. Possibly mistaking the Beaufighters for torpedo-bomber Beauforts, some ships protected their sides by turning bows on to the low-level attack and were strafed from end to end by the heavily armed fighters. Four cannon in the nose and six guns in the wings gave the Beaufighter formidable fire power which ripped into superstructure and silenced much of the destroyers' anti-aircraft fire. The Beaufighters were followed by the Mitchells, a more heavily armed version of the earlier B-25s. The mediums caused the most damage, mainly through the use of the new skip-bombing technique first experimented with by the RAF and practised in the Fifth Air Force under General Kenney's instruction. The Mitchells scored seventeen direct hits in conventional and skip-bombing attacks, littering the sea with sinking and burning ships. A Beaufighter shot down a Zero attacking a Mitchell and although a couple of Allied aircraft, apart from the three Lightnings and the Fortress, were damaged, the entire force was able to retire intact to rearm and refuel.

Fortresses, Mitchells, Bostons and

Beaufighters, escorted by Lightnings, attacked again during the afternoon, when a greater number of skip-bombing hits were scored. Zeros intercepted but the attacking force returned safely. That night five American MTBs from Tufi found a crippled ship and sank it with torpedoes and by the following morning the only target left was a damaged destroyer, easily sunk by the returning bombers. The Malahang airfield near Lae was raided by Lightnings, bombers and Beaufighters, shooting up everything in sight without loss except for a Beaufighter later destroyed in a crash-landing at Dobadura, the crew escaping unhurt.

Lieutenant-Commander Handa later described the attack on Admiral Kimura's flagship *Shirayuki:* '... waves of three planes which came in at extremely low level ... in strafing and bombing attacks. Most personnel on the bridge were killed or wounded (the Admiral was wounded). A bomb hit the after turret ... a fire started, a powder magazine exploded, and the stern section broke off and the ship was flooded and sank.' The crew were transferred to the destroyer *Shikinami* which, with three other destroyers, picked up some 2,700 survivors from the sunken ships,

transferring them later to ships summoned from Rabaul and met east of Long Island. The destroyers had escaped unnoticed by the Allied airmen who believed they had sunk the entire convoy. Nevertheless it was an outstanding success which pleased even MacArthur. He later described it as being the decisive aerial engagement of the war in the South-West Pacific.

Rafts, barges and ships' boats carrying survivors were unmercifully strafed during the following days. Any Japanese troops reaching land would have reinforced the enemy facing the Allied ground forces. Nearly 3,000 Japanese army troops, marines and seamen were killed or drowned in the sinking of the twelve ships. Many enemy aircraft were shot down or destroyed on the Lae strips while the Allied losses were those already mentioned, plus a Mitchell lost in an accident, and thirteen aircrew killed. The Allied Air Force had forcibly demonstrated its superiority in the SWPA and from now on the enemy in New Guinea were cut off from supplies by sea except for slow and inadequate deliveries made by submarines which surfaced at night in the bays, and by hazardous coast-hugging runs made by camouflaged barges.

Birth of the P-40

The ancestral name of Hawk aircraft comes from Kitty Hawk in North Carolina, known throughout the world as the birthplace of powered flight. On 4th September 1903, in the Kill Devil Hills four miles south of the town, Wilbur Wright won the toss from his brother Orville and took off in their 'Flyer' biplane from a launching rail laid downhill into wind. The Wright-designed engine powered the 'Flyer' into a steep climb ending in a stall and a crash into the sand. So ended the first flight, made with too much up-elevator, witnessed by some of the Wrights' friends from the Kill Devil Hills Life Saving Station. On 17th December it was Orville's turn to take the controls, flying off the rail from level ground and staying in the air for about twelve seconds, covering 120 feet at a speed of 30 mph on the first flight and, on the fourth flight that morning, increasing this to 852 feet. At last, after centuries of wishful thinking by would-be fliers, powered flight had proven feasible.

During the First World War aircraft manufacturers on both sides were forced into the race to build better performing, more powerful machines with reliable motors. Germany, France and Britain produced both in-line and radial engines, and one of the best and most reliable was the Rolls-Royce 'Eagle' which could run for 150 hours between overhauls. The 'Eagle' was a twelve-cylinder Vee, displacing 20.32 litres, improving in power output from 225hp at 1,800rpm in 1915, to 360hp at 2,000rpm by 1918. The successful performance of the Rolls-Royce engine influenced many aircraft designers, on both sides of the Atlantic, who preferred the low-drag qualities of an in-line to the lower-weight benefit of a radial power unit, so design their airframes to accomodate liquid-cooled V-12 engines. The engineers predicted enormous power

possibilities in future developments of this type of motor, vindicated by the successes in Schneider Trophy races of short-life V-12s developing 2,000hp.

The first time Americans entered the Schneider Trophy contests they walked away with the event. The year before, 1922, the Royal Aero Club had taken the prize with their Supermarine Sea Lion II entrant, a radial-engined pusher biplane flying-boat designed by R J Mitchell. With modified hull and clipped wings, Sea Lion III flew for the Royal Aero Club at the contest held at Cowes, Isle of Wight, when Curtiss CR3 racers challenged. One, flown by Lieutenant David Rittenhouse, achieved an average speed of 177.38mph, 26mph faster than Sea Lion. It could well be that the use of an in-line V-12 motor in Rittenhouse's Curtiss Racer biplane influenced Mitchell to use that type of motor to power his mono-seaplanes, which eventually won the Trophy outright for the RAC and which were the ancestors to the Spitfire. The next contest after Rittenhouse's victory was held in America and again victory went to a Curtiss Racer, this time entered by the army and flown by Lieutenant James Doolittle. There was no test against the Mitchell S.4 seaplane, which crashed, but the Curtiss Racer's average speed of 232.5mph over the triangular course would have been difficult to better. There was never any further competition between these two ancestors of famous Second World War fighters.

While the Spitfire, first flown in 1936, was Supermarine's only fighter type to be built by that company, the Curtiss Aeroplane and Motor Company of Buffalo and Garden City, New York, built fighters, both airframes and engines, for the US Army and Navy a couple of years after the end of the First World War, and during that war had built large numbers of Jenny trainers. By 1918 the Curtiss water-cooled V-12 engine had been successfully introduced, its developed power

The slim XP-40Q-2, coming at the end of the P-40 line, was too late to see active service

Above : Originally a French contract Hawk 75A-4, this model became Mohawk IV in RAF service. *Below :* Tomahawk II of No 3 Squadron RAAF, Libya 1941

of 435hp coming from a displacement of 1,150 cubic inches. Hotted-up versions of this motor, the Kirkham-Curtiss D-12, later designated V-1150, powered the Racers built for the army and navy between 1921 and 1925. In these aircraft water cooling was effected by leading the water tubes flat across the upper surfaces of the top wings. From racers emerged the PW-8 (Pursuit, Water-cooled) fighter, a trim, single-seater ordered by the US Air Service – later US Air Corps – in 1923. The fuselage and divided-axle undercarriage were of tubular steel construction and the wings were made from laminated plywood. One of these aircraft, the XPW-8B, produced with a tunnel radiator which had been tested in an army design of 1920, and with tapered wings, became the prototype for a new line of fighters which were known as the Curtiss 'Hawk'.

In 1925 the US Army ordered fifteen Curtiss P-1 Hawks, armed with either two .30-inch machine guns or one .30-inch and one .50-inch, the two guns synchronised to fire through the propeller. Service models and experimental models, to P-6E and XP-23, were produced in a great variety of types until 1938 and were the best known American fighter in the prewar years. Curtiss tested various radial and in-line engines in similar fuselages, guns mounted in cowlings and guns mounted on the wings, the aircraft having enclosed canopies and fixed undercarriages. Until 1929 the Army continued to enter its Hawks in air races, particularly the National Air Race, to publicise the Air Corps and make comparisons with other aircraft. The end product of these years of development was the P-6E, powered by the new 700hp Conqueror V-1510 and possessing a maximum sea-level speed of 198mph. The last production P-6E Hawk completed, the XP-23, was given a pointed nose shape to the engine cowling and, with the deep radiator housing positioned underneath the engine, the general fuselage shape of the future fighters

was outlined. In Army exercises the planes were painted in camouflage colours, otherwise they were given yellow wings and empennage with the exception of a blue vertical stripe and red and white horizontal stripes on the rudder, and at first a khaki, but later an olive drab fuselage.

Before the war the Hawks and other American fighters were hardly any faster than the well-armed bombers; the Air Corps seemed content with the developments taking place at the Bell and Curtiss aircraft factories where the Airacobra and future Hawks were evolving. There had been a precedent in the US of low-wing monoplanes serving with the Air Corps. Its first all-metal single-seater fighter with retractable undercarriage was the Seversky P-35, delivered in 1937, the year in which the Bf 109B and the Hurricane I also went into service. The following year Curtiss delivered the P-36 which had first appeared in prototype form in 1935. After poor initial performance, as a result of which a production order was placed with Seversky, the P-36 was re-engined and now performed better than the Seversky design, and the government approved an Air Corps expenditure in ordering 210 Curtiss fighters in July 1937.

Don Berlin, Chief Engineer of the Curtiss Wright Corporation Airplane Division, as the company was now called, led the design team who built the P-36. They gave it a radial engine, initially a Wright XR-1670-5, replaced by a Pratt & Whitney R-1830-13 Twin Wasp, a monocoque fuselage, a fully retractable undercarriage, hydraulically-operated split-flaps and a Hamilton-Standard three-blade constant-speed airscrew. It was the world's first fighter to have a retractable tailwheel. Although considered obsolete and used primarily for advanced training in 1940, P-36As were in action at Pearl Harbor on the fateful 7th December 1941. They also saw action in Europe. When the US Government released them for export, Hawk H75As, as they were designated by the company, were sold to France in 1938 and 1939. Known as the Mohawk in the Royal Air Force, to which the Hawk H75As meant for France were delivered after the fall of that country, the fighter also operated in the Middle East. The export P-36s were fitted with Pratt & Whitney R-1830 Twin Wasp radials and Wright R-1830 Cyclone radials, which developed 1,050hp and 1,200hp respectively, reaching a top speed of 311mph and 323 mph at 10,000 feet and 15,000 feet. At 20,000 feet, to which height they could climb in 8.8 minutes, their speed was 10 mph less. Service ceiling was between 33,700 and 32,700 feet respectively and economical cruising range 960 miles at 130mph. They could carry 400lbs weight of bombs in under-wing racks and armament was up to four 7.5mm machine guns in the wings as well as two 7.5mm guns in the cowling. Many French Mohawks were shot down or destroyed on the ground by the German air force but several won victories over Me 109s. Four units of the Armée de l'Air equipped with Mohawks shot down more than 240 enemy aircraft and if French military leadership had not been so generally inefficient fewer aircraft would have been lost on the ground and fighters and fighter-bombers could have slowed down the Panzer divisions. Captured Mohawks were flown by the Finns in action against Russia and while some of the French Hawks were flown to Britain when France fell, others remained there for use by the Vichy government. Other countries to buy or build under licence P-36s were Norway, Canada, Peru, India, Portugal, Iran, China, South Africa, Thailand and Argentina. Argentina set up a factory which built 200 under licence, commencing in 1940.

The next major development of the Hawk was the P-40, whose prototype was built around the airframe of a P-36A. The power unit was the new V-12 in-line liquid-cooled engine built by the Allison Division of General Motors Corporation, manufacturers of aircraft engines since 1930. The V-12 type of motor had been much more in demand by the RAF for fighters and bombers than in the US Army Air Corps, which showed a preference for radial motors. However, the new Allison produced such good results in its marriage to the Curtiss airframe that the USAAC were impressed by the XP-40, as it was designated.

The order for the experimental machine was issued in July 1937 and the XP-40's first flight took place fifteen months later. It was hardly a momentous occasion, since Curtiss had flown many of their tested and proved aircraft with different engines, yet the success of this new combination was to have far-reaching effects in the conduct of the aerial war to come, both in its original fighter role and later as a workhorse of the Second World War. With the Bell Airacobra, the Allison-powered fighters provided more than half the USAAF fighter strength up to July 1943.

The Curtiss wing was retained in its P-36 shape, the underneath section rising sharply near the tip to give the P-40 its characteristic turned-up wing appearance. The span of 37 feet 4 inches and wing area of 236 square feet were to remain the same in all future models. Maximum speed of 342mph was attained at the comparatively low height of 12,200 feet, much too low for effective combat against the latest German fighter types. Protective armour had been tried out in pursuit aircraft in 1918, but the extra weight hampered performance too much and was discarded. Experience in Europe was to render essential armour plate fitted behind the cockpit, and this was made a standard requirement for all US fighters after 1940. Curtiss had fitted quarter-inch plate in their P-40s in 1939. Leak-proof fuel tanks had also been tested in 1918 but were not fitted until 1940. The Allison V-1710-19 (C-13) engine developed 1,000hp at 10,000 feet and 1,160hp at ground level for take-off, ratings that were not quite

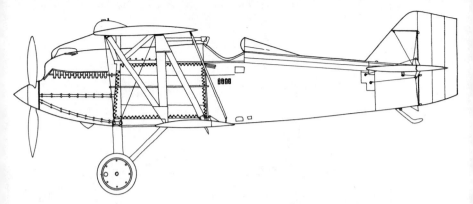

Curtiss PW-8

Developed from the Curtiss series of racing aircraft, the PW-8 was delivered to the USAAC during 1924. As befitted an aircraft derived from a racer, it was very well streamlined. The designation PW indicates that the aircraft was in the Pursuit class and was powered by a water-cooled engine. *Engine :* Curtiss D-12, **440hp** *Armament :* two .30-inch machine guns with 600 rounds per gun, or one .30-inch and one .50-inch machine guns, the .50-inch gun having 200 rounds *Maximum speed :* 162mph at 6,500 feet. *Climb :* 10,000 feet in 9 minutes *Ceiling :* 23,300 feet. *Range :* 440 miles. *Weight empty/loaded :* 2,191lbs/3,151lbs *Span :* 32 feet. *Length :* 22 feet 6 inches

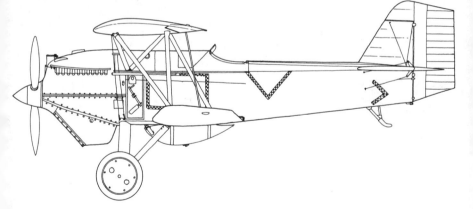

Curtiss P-1C

The next Curtiss fighter after the PW-8 to go into production, the P-1 series of Hawk fighters were well liked by their pilots. It was found, however, that the increases in weight in this model were having an adverse effect on performance The C version of the basic P-1 was fitted with wheel brakes. *Engine :* Curtiss V-1150-5, 435hp. *Armament :* two .30-inch machine guns. *Maximum speed :* 154mph at sea level. *Climb :* 10,000 feet in 9.1 minutes. *Ceiling :* 22,300 feet. *Range :* 550 miles *Weight empty/loaded :* 2,136lbs/2,973lbs. *Span :* 31 feet 6 inches. *Length :* 23 feet 3 inches

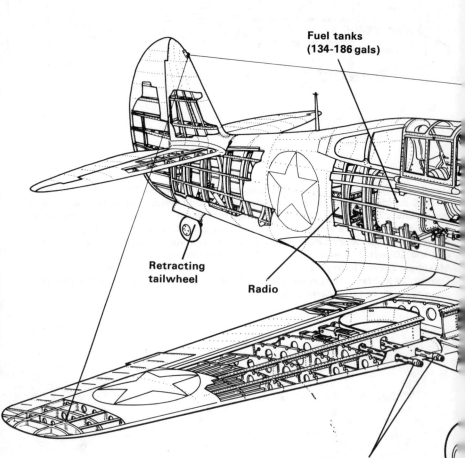

Fuel tanks
(134-186 gals)

Retracting
tailwheel

Radio

.30 machine guns

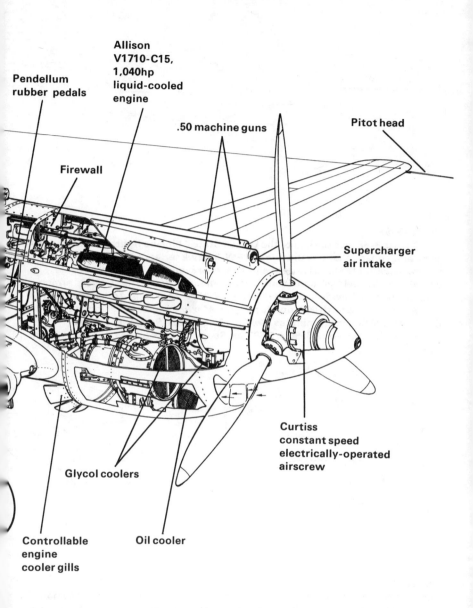

Pendellum
rubber pedals

Allison
V1710-C15,
1,040hp
liquid-cooled
engine

.50 machine guns

Pitot head

Firewall

Supercharger
air intake

Curtiss
constant speed
electrically-operated
airscrew

Glycol coolers

Controllable
engine
cooler gills

Oil cooler

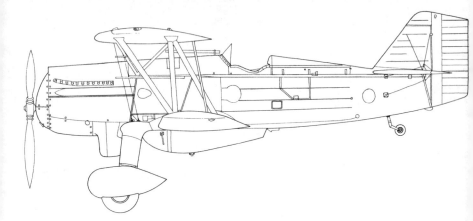

Curtiss P-6E
The Curtiss P-6E was the last of the United States' biplane fighters. Still having the same empennage shape as the original PW-8 Hawk series of fighters, this last Hawk was far superior to the original of eight years previously, with its droppable 50-gallon belly fuel tank and a cantilevered undercarriage. The standard armament was still carried, however. *Engine :* Curtiss V-1570-23, 600hp. *Armament :* two .30-inch machine guns with 600 rounds per gun. *Maximum speed :* 198mph at sea level *Climb :* 10,000 feet in 5.3 minutes. *Ceiling :* 25,800 feet. *Range :* 572 miles *Weight empty/loaded :* 2,699lbs/3,392lbs. *Span :* 31 feet 6 inches. *Length :* 23 feet 2 inches

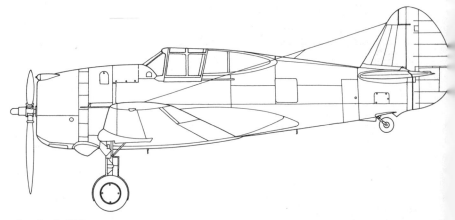

Curtiss P-36A
The Curtiss P-36A (Curtiss Design Number 75) was conceived as a replacement for the Army Air Corps' ageing Boeing P-26 fighter, and first appeared in March 1937 It was an advanced aircraft for its time in the USA with a retractable undercarriage and fully enclosed cockpit, but was still not up to date with the latest European designs. *Engine :* Pratt & Whitney R-1830-13 Twin Wasp, 1,050hp. *Armament :* one .30-inch machine gun with 600 rounds and one .50-inch machine gun with 200 rounds *Maximum speed :* 300mph at 10,000 feet. *Climb :* 15,000 feet in 4.9 minutes *Ceiling :* 33,000 feet. *Range :* 825 miles. *Weight empty/loaded :* 4,567lbs/6,010lbs *Span :* 37 feet 4 inches. *Length :* 28 feet 6 inches

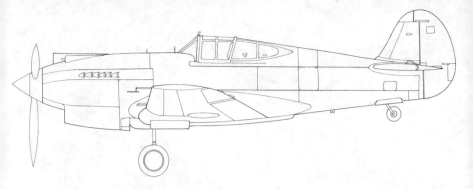

Curtiss P-40B
Engine : Allison V-1710-33, 1,150hp. *Armament :* two .50-inch and two .30-inch machine guns. *Maximum speed :* 352mph at 15,000 feet. *Climb :* 15,000 feet in 5.1 minutes. *Ceiling :* 32,400 feet. *Range :* 945 miles. *Weight empty/loaded :* 5,590lbs/7,600lbs. *Span :* 37 feet 4 inches. *Length :* 31 feet 9 inches

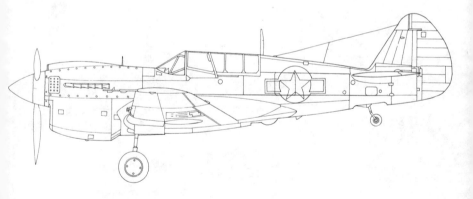

Curtiss P-40N Warhawk
Engine : Allison V-1710-81, 1,200hp. *Armament :* six .50-inch machine guns and three 500lb bombs. *Maximum speed :* 343mph at 15,000 feet. *Climb :* 20,000 feet in 8.8 minutes. *Ceiling :* 31,000 feet. *Range :* 1,080 miles. *Weight empty/loaded :* 6,200lbs/11,400lbs. *Span :* 37 feet 4 inches. *Length :* 33 feet 4 inches

Above: Arming a RAAF Kittyhawk's 500lb bomb. *Below:* Clive Caldwell on the wing of the Spitfire which bears his initials. *Right:* Members of 112 Squadron

adequate for the requirements of a modern fighter.

Although no doubt the USAAC was constantly evaluating the experimental fighters being developed at Lockheed (XP-38 Lightning), Bell (XP-39 Airacobra), Seversky (XP-41 and AP-4) and Curtiss (75R, XP-37 and XP-42), an Army Pursuit Contest was organised and held at Wright Field in May 1939, to choose the aircraft which came up to Army specifications for the award of an order to manufacture. Despite the failure of the XP-40 to fulfil some of the requirements for performance, modest compared with the original hopes of the USAAC for 400mph at 20,000 feet, Curtiss received an order to mass-produce their fighter, mainly because they were the only manufacturers in a position to rush into large-scale production. The first

order, placed on 27th April 1939, was for 524 modified P-40 pursuits, at a price of about $22,500 each, and first deliveries were made in May 1940.

The main modification to the first prototype design was the installation of a more powerful engine produced by Allison, the supercharged V-1710-33 (C-15), which was rated at 1,040hp at 15,000 feet. This performance was still too low by European standards but the maximum speed at that height satisfied the Air Corps who did not anticipate the combats which were to rage at heights of 20,000 to 30,000 feet. The twin radiators for the ethelyne-glycol coolant, in a housing which also accommodated the oil-cooler, was moved forward to just under the nose from behind the wing trailing edge. The first models possessed only the old arrangement of guns firing through the airscrew. The plane's length was 31 feet 8¾ inches and height, to tip of airscrew, was 10 feet 7 inches. Weight was 5,376lbs empty, 6,787lbs gross and 7,215lbs maximum loaded, weights which were to increase with extra armament and equipment, and lower the maximum speed from 357mph to 345mph, when it went into service with the RAF as the Tomahawk I. The first foreign orders were from France but the French machines, with French instruments and cockpit lettering, and without cockpit armour, bullet-proof windscreens or self-sealing tanks, were diverted to the RAF and became advanced trainers.

In the RAF the P-40B was named Tomahawk IIA and the more combat-worthy P-40C (Curtiss H81-A-2) became the Tomahawk IIB. The shape of the nose, which suggested a shark's profile, more pronounced in later model P-40s, led to a squadron artist of 112 Squadron, RAF, to paint the famous

Left : Fitting dust cover to a Tomahawk.
Below : On this kind of 'airfield' the covers were clearly necessary

'shark's teeth' insignia on the radiator housing, from underneath the spinner back towards the wing root. When the 'Flying Tigers', the American Volunteer Group in China, received their P-40s, they too added shark's teeth to bite at the enemy.

In China the P-40s destroyed six out of ten bombers in their first action on 20th December 1941. It was in China that the first tactics for the slow-climbing, heavy fighter were worked out by Chennault. These laid down the cardinal rules for fighting the highly maneouvrable Zero. The new P-40Bs (there was no A) were armed with two .50-inch machine guns in the cowling and two or four .30-inch guns in the wings and the P-40C with four .30-inch guns in the wings. Maximum loading went up to 8,058lbs with bigger, self-sealing tanks, the extra guns and ammunition, cockpit armour and radios. Altogether, 930 Tomahawk IIBs (P-40C) were built for the RAF. RAF Tomahawks had .303-inch rather than .30-inch guns.

Exhibiting that peculiar military trait of resistance to new inventions, Colonel Foch declared in 1911: 'The

aeroplane is good sport, but worthless for use by the army.' By 1915 he had been proved wrong. The aeroplane was important for reconnaissance and some ground-support work in that war, and was invaluable in a multiplicity of roles in its modern form (beginning with Mussolini's invasion of Abyssinia and the Spanish Civil War), in aiding the needs of the army in the Second World War. During 1941, Tomahawks proved their toughness through months of constant operations in the Western Desert where the oscillating movement of armies forced the RAF to use rough and dusty aerodromes from which they could satisfy the army's requirements for close support. As interceptors Tomahawks were limited, yet in the hands of skilful fighter pilots like Clive 'Killer' Caldwell, RAAF, and Neville Duke, RAF, superior machines, such as the Bf 109, were shot down as well as the inferior Regia Aeronautica fighters. Caldwell shot down over twenty enemy aircraft while flying P-40s in the Desert.

Maximum speed of the Desert Air Forces' P-40C Tomahawk IIB was 345mph at 15,000 feet, cruising speed was 270mph and landing speed 85mph. Three main tanks held 148 Imperial gallons of fuel, 35 gallons in the front section of the wings, 50.5 in the main section and 62.5 in the fuselage tanks. Range was normally 730 miles, increased to 1,230 miles with a 52-gallon auxiliary tank, at economical cruising speed, and service ceiling was 29,500 feet. Rate of climb was best at 5,000 feet – 2,650 feet per minute. These performance figures are much lower than for the P-40A and P-40B, owing solely to increases in weight. The three-blade variable-pitch Curtiss airscrew was operated electrically and was, surprisingly in a fighter, capable of being fully-feathered.

The robustness of the P-40's undercarriage enabled the aircraft to land on rough surfaces and plough through thick dust in the desert or the slop that covered the strip at Milne Bay.

The large wheels, attached to Curtiss oleo-pneumatic shock-absorber legs, retracted backwards and rotated through ninety degrees to fit flush into the wing recesses; the tail wheel not only retracted but was steerable and was covered in the 'up' position by twin door flaps.

Occasionally when Tomahawks were forced to land on the desert they landed wheels down, but only after a close examination of the desert floor, if that were possible, and most of such landings were successfully made on the rough terrain. One of the most severe tests to a P-40's undercarriage was made by Squadron Leader Bobby Gibbes DSO, DFC and Bar, commander of 3 Squadron RAAF. One of his men was forced down in the desert near the German lines and Gibbes circled around to gauge whether the terrain was smooth and level enough to make a rescue landing. The downed pilot's radio was still working and he warned his CO that the ground was too rough. However, Gibbes, decided to risk it to save his man from a POW camp, landed safely and picked him up. Taking off with a passenger in the cockpit was difficult enough without having to get the P-40 up from a run of about 300 yards over ridges. It bounced badly a couple of times and blew a tyre, just missed a third ridge but stayed airborne. Arriving back over the base they were forced to make a belly-landing, but the P-40 held together without either pilot being injured. Once Gibbes was shot down, after tackling three Me 109s and shooting one of them down, and was forced to walk back to his own lines through enemy territory, at one time having to hide in a wadi while a German motorised column drove past him. He was rescued by advancing troops after three days. Gibbes shot down at least eleven enemy aircraft in the Desert and flew 450 operational hours during his service there.

The P-40 appeared to be at home in the desert where it produced valuable results. Behind its success, of course,

German and Italian wreckage in the Western Desert. *Above:* Ju 87B-2.
Below: Fiat CR.42

Left : AVG machines in Burma
Below left : No. 3 Squadron Tomahawk
Below : Hawk 75A-3 of Vichy Air Force
Bottom : No. 120 Squadron Kittyhawks
operating from Biak, New Guinea,
carrying long-range tanks

AVG pilots of 1st Pursuit Squadron race for their planes (Hawk 81 A-3s)

**Adjusting the ammunition feed
mechanism of 'Cleo', a Tomahawk in
service in the Western Desert**

was the enormous effort of ground
crews to keep the air filters clean and
carry out all the dozens of other
routine maintenance jobs in the open,
where desert climatic conditions often
made such work intolerable, dust
being the worst infliction on man and
machine. And success was achieved
also by the astounding skill and guts
of many of the pilots who had to fly
it against the far superior Me 109.
Pilots in the Desert, as in New Guinea,
very often attacked escorted enemy
bombers first, offering an advantage
to their fighter escort. Several
squadrons operated in the Western
Desert with Curtiss planes during
1941 and 1942, notably 94, 112, 250

and 260 Squadrons RAF, 3 and 450
Squadrons RAAF, and 5 and 7 Squadrons South African Air Force. When
the two veteran squadrons, 3 RAAF and
112 RAF, first exchanged their Gloster
Gladiator fixed-undercarriage
biplanes for P-40s, several pilots made
wheels-up landings, forgetting the
undercarriage lever in their landing
approach cockpit drill. The sturdy
machines not only protected the
pilots; repairs to the damage were not
too difficult to carry out in the desert
workshops. Combat against the
Italian fighters was even feasible with
the old Gladiators but with increased
numbers of German fighters arriving
in North Africa the need for modern
fighters became desperate. Some Hurricanes had been sent from Britain and
Spitfires were promised. Meanwhile
the air forces wore out their Toma-

hawks as they waited for the improved P-40, the model D which the RAF would designate Kittyhawk.

Some Tomahawk pilots had come from air fighting over Britain while others were inexperienced trainees fresh from OTUs. Clive Caldwell DSO, DFC and two Bars, Polish Cross of Valour, first flew Hurricanes in the Desert then, in 250 Squadron, Tomahawks during the Syrian campaign where the fighting was confused by the fact that Vichy forces flew Mohawks marked with roundels. When the squadron returned to the Desert, Caldwell was a flight commander, leading missions against the Axis forces, fighter sweeps and bomber escorts to Gazala, Gambut, El Adem, Sidi Hameish, Sollum, Bardia, Benghazi, defensive patrols over coastal shipping, tactical reconnaissances and strafing at dawn and sunset along the Axis front lines. In one clash with Me 109s he won a victory while wounded. Weaving alone as lookout above the squadron on convoy patrol over the Gulf of Sollum, he was jumped by two Messerschmitts making a simultaneous attack in which they shot off an aileron, damaged both wings, smashed the cockpit canopy and wrecked part of the instrument panel. He was wounded in shoulder, legs and back, sprayed with hot oil, and found himself in a spin. Yet he managed to pull out and give battle to the Germans. He shot one down and the other fled. Caldwell landed safely, one tyre punctured, at Sidi Barrani.

Such fighting ability negates the comparative performance statistics of fighter aircraft. By knowing the capabilities of one's own aircraft, being able to shoot with an uncanny eye and being quick and aggressive, plus, as Chennault said, use of the right tactic, it was always possible to shoot down the average enemy pilot in a superior machine.

Like John Jackson, Caldwell was old for a fighter pilot; he had passed his thirtieth birthday when he became the first Allied fighter pilot to shoot down five enemy machines in one combat, creating another record by getting two of them in one burst. It happened while he was the commander of 112 Squadron and was leading nineteen P-40s from 112 and 250 squadrons on patrol over forward troops east of El Adem. Warned by Control of a large group of enemy aircraft in the vicinity, about one hundred of them were found, mixed formations of Me 109s, Macchi 202s and Ju 87 Stukas. Caldwell led two sections of P-40s into the enemy fighters head-on, then after they had been split up he found a formation of three Stukas flying tight in a staggered port echelon. He made a quarter beam attack from slightly below, his burst of fire hit both number two and number three Stukas, the first blowing up and the second going down in flames. Twenty-four of the enemy were shot down in that fight, a high recommendation for the old Tomahawks.

A month later, another Tomahawk pilot, New Zealand-born 'Nicky' Barr, demonstrated that even when heavily handicapped the Tomahawk could cause a lot of damage. Attacked by German and Italian fighters while escorting bombers south of Benghazi, Barr tackled two Macchis, shooting one down, then shot down a Messerschmitt that had just shot down another P-40. It was enemy territory and Barr decided to land in the desert to rescue the pilot. He was in the vulnerable position of approaching to land with wheels and flaps down when two Me 109s attacked. He shot one down before they got him. He crash-landed and was wounded as he escaped from the wreckage. After three days he arrived back in the British lines, wearing Arab dress and riding a camel. Barr also won two DFCs and could unofficially wear the emblem of the 'Flying Boot Club' after escaping from a German POW train in Italy and walking back to Allied lines. He had again been shot down in the desert, this time in a Kittyhawk, and, wounded and burned, had been captured.

Kittyhawks

The P-40D, P-40E, P-40F, P-40K, P-40M and P-40N series were designated Kittyhawk I, IA, II, III and IV in RAF and Commonwealth air forces – including the Dutch whose P-40 squadrons operated under Australian control in the SWPA. In the USAAF these aircraft were known as the Warhawk, also thus named in accounts of its service in Chinese and Russian air forces.

In spite of a lack of some of the refinements possessed by contemporary enemy and Allied fighters, which were radically modified for a multiplicity of specialised uses, the P-40 basic design was retained in its new and improved versions. The RAAF was satisfied enough with the performance of the Tomahawk to order, before one had flown, 560 of the newer model, the P-40D, or Kittyhawk I. Curtiss had been studying the possibilities of building the best qualities of foreign fighters into their experimental XP-46 which would be powered by the new Allison V-1710-39 engine rated at 1,150hp at take-off and 11,700 feet. The XP-46 was to have carried ten machine guns and flown at over 400mph. However, it was found that necessary extras increased the weight and brought the performance of the experimental fighter, a smaller version of the P-40 with an inward retracting undercarriage, to only a little better than that of a P-40C. Therefore it was decided that, by fitting the more

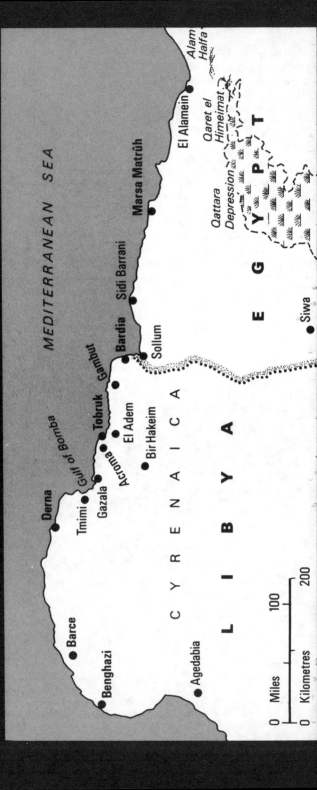

powerful Allison to a slightly redesigned Hawk airframe, a useful fighter would result and valuable time would be saved in production at the aircraft factories.

By May 1941, when the P-40D prototype was taken up on its maiden flight, German troops and aircraft were strongly entrenched in North Africa, and Britain was necessarily conserving her fighters for a possible second defensive air battle over her cities and airfields. It was one of the many times during the first three years of the war when miracles were asked for, and the not so small miracle of American manufacturing techniques rushed the P-40s from Curtiss production lines. The extent of Curtiss Airplane Division expansion was a measure of the demand for the fighter: numbers of aircraft workers increased to 45,000 during 1941 when the plants increased in area by 400 per cent to over four and a quarter million square feet. Original production was centred at Buffalo where a second plant was built, another was built at Columbus, Ohio, and the Curtiss St Louis plant was expanded. When all of these plants were eventually working at top speed, sixty new P-40s a day were ready for flight testing.

In the air, the profile view of the Tomahawk showed more graceful lines than those of the Kittyhawk which appeared, in straight and level flight, to be endeavouring to climb but was too heavy to make it. The Kittyhawk's nose was shorter, the total length reduced to 31 feet 2 inches and the deeper radiator had been enlarged and moved forward. The oleo legs were shortened slightly. Six .50-inch machine guns were fitted in the wings as standard armament for all air forces, although the first twenty received into the RAF late in 1941 were fitted with only four guns. Thus there was a quick change of model designation: the four-gun machine was the P-40D and the six-gun the P-40E or E-I, known in the RAF as Kittyhawk I. Those supplied until Lend-Lease were

known as Kittyhawk IAs. The M-3 machine gun weighed 52 pounds and fired a round weighing 1.71 ounces at a muzzle velocity of 2,500 feet per second and at a rate of 1,100 rounds per minute, with a range of nearly 7,000 yards. For aerial combat the best range was up to 200 yards and the guns were aligned so that their fire converged at this distance. America's allies purchased these aircraft through the Lend-Lease arrangement. The total number of P-40Es produced was 2,320.

At 15,000 feet, its best operating height, the Kittyhawk IA could fly at a maximum speed of only 354mph and climb to that height in 8.3 minutes, a longer time than the A6M2 Zero took to reach 20,000 feet. Empty weight was 6,350 pounds, normal loaded weight 8,280 pounds, which was the load carried into combat without drop tank or bombs, and maximum permissible weight was 9,200 pounds. Service ceiling was 29,000 feet. The IA climbed best at lower altitudes, but its best rate was only about 2,100 feet per minute at 5,000 feet. Over 10,000 feet, which could be reached in about 4.8 minutes, pilots used an oxygen 'bladder' mask, unlike the normal RAF mask which incorporated the radio microphone; the US microphone was a light attachment at the pilot's throat which picked up voice vibrations, and were thus called 'throat mikes'.

Tomahawks in the Desert Air Force were replaced by Kittyhawks from January 1942, the time when, during the see-saw land battles in the Desert, it was Rommel's turn to advance and the British ground forces were having a tough time withdrawing back towards Egypt. The support squadrons moved back with them, using temporary airfields when defensive stands were made by the army and sometimes having to abandon slow-moving workshop vehicles. 112 Squadron was one of several in the fighter force engaged mainly on ground support duties and escorting medium bombers.

And there were Messerschmitt Bf 109s to be warily avoided unless height, sun and numbers gave the Kittyhawk pilots a reasonable chance against superior German machines. As in Europe, the Luftwaffe pilots flew high, and Allied pilots in the Desert were also advised 'beware of the Hun in the sun'.

Sergeant Leu of 112 Squadron won the first Kittyhawk victory over an enemy aircraft in North Africa. On 25th January his aircraft was one of a flight of nine flying close escort to Blenheim bombers on a raid to Agedabia. Five Me 109s attacked them on the journey home and Leu turned head on to one, severely damaging its wing with a burst of fire; then the enemy plane was seen to crash. Sometimes the fighting was hit-or-miss and dive away, but mostly the clashes occurred because one or other of the groups of fighters wanted to stop bombers under escort. This extract from 112 Squadron's history describes an action which took place in the month following Sergeant Leu's victory:

'Nos 3 and 75 Squadrons were also there to act as top cover, but four of these were obliged to return to base with engine trouble for a start. What were left were intercepted by three Messerschmitt Bf 109s, and one Kittyhawk was shot down and another so badly damaged that it barely returned to Gambut. The enemy flew off before they could be engaged and in the confusion five more Kittyhawks lost contact with the Blenheims. There was a rearguard fight and three pilots – Sergeant-Pilots Elwell, Donkin and Hoare – failed to return. One Me 109F flew a parallel course to the bombers out to starboard to act as decoy, and Flight-Lieutenant Humphreys managed to get in an attack on him.

'The Me 109s then started a series of "dive and away" tactics. Sergeant-Pilot Burney finished off the decoy near Bomba, and also saw a Messerschmitt and a Kittyhawk crash into the sea about twenty yards apart, east

of the Gulf of Bomba. Sergeant-Pilot Elwell and Sergeant-Pilot Hoare were almost certainly shot down, and one of them took a Me 109 witn him. The score was one Me 109F destroyed by Sergeant-Pilot Burney, one Me 109F destroyed by an unknown pilot and one more shared between Flight-Lieutenant Humphreys and Sergeant-Pilot Burney. Total – three-all.'

It is obvious that no aces were involved in this action yet the P-40s equalled the score with the German fighter which was over thirty miles an hour faster, could turn tighter and could climb to 10,000 feet in under three minutes. With large reserves of pilots training at Empire Air Training Scheme depots throughout the world by 1942, graduating pilots could spend more time at Operational Training Units to learn from war-experienced instructors the correct way to fly the P-40 in action, to fight with 'the best characteristic' of the plane, and learn how to avoid being shot down. Chance, too, always played a large part in a fighter clash, yet in the big mix-up of

14th February some new pilots fought with the old hands, without losing one Kittyhawk, to win an outstanding victory against the best, Me 109Fs, and worst, Macchi 200s, fighters the enemy had in North Africa at the time. The Macchi MC 200 'Seatta' was a radial-engine interceptor that reached 313 mph at 14,770 feet, climbed and turned well but was lightly armed with two 12.7mm Safat machine guns in the fuselage. The Macchi MC 202 'Folgore' was a much improved machine, with an Italian-built Daimler-Benz DB 601A in-line engine that gave the plane a top speed of 370mph at 16,400 feet, a climb to 19,685 feet in 5 minutes 55 seconds, and armament increased by two 7.7mm machine guns in the wings. The good manoeuvrability of the MC 200 was retained in the MC 202.

This is what happened on the 14th: 'Ten Kittyhawks led by Pilot Officer Bartle with Sergeant-Pilot Simonsen, Pilot Officer Duke, Sergeant-Pilot Leu, Pilot Officer Dickenson, Sergeant-Pilot Evans, Sergeant-Pilot Drew, Sergeant-Pilot Christie, Ser-

23rd Fighter Group 14th Air Force in China. A Hawk receives beauty treatment

geant-Pilot Cordwell, Sergeant-Pilot Burney and eight aircraft from No 3 Squadron RAAF, were scrambled to meet an approaching enemy formation. After flying north to Tobruk the Kittyhawks turned west over the perimeter defences and climbed steadily until, over Acroma, No 3 Squadron were flying at 8,000 feet with 112 slightly ahead and above, just below the cloud base, and an ideal height for the Kittyhawk. At this moment, they spotted about a dozen MC 202s and C 202s in a loose vic formation, 2,000 feet below them, to the left and in front. Pilot Officer Bartle warned the Australians, who had, however, already seen a formation of enemy bombers, with close cover escort (Me 109s), flying at less than 2,000 feet. The 112 pilots concentrated on the fighters who now were climbing to meet the attack. The enemies' courage failed them and they hurriedly tried to form a defensive circle, in a half-hearted fashion. The Kittyhawks dived into them and in the initial attack every aircraft must have hit something. Sergeant-Pilot Burney, having dived through the formation, saw the bombers below; they were BR 65s, and so he carried on down and shot one down. By the time he regained the formation there were no enemy fighters to be seen among the milling Kittyhawks.

'Sergeant-Pilot Cordwell, in his first action, shot away about three-quarters of the wing of a Me 109F, which spun in out of control. Sergeant-Pilot Evans attacked an MC 200 as it was turning and shot about two feet off its starboard wing. It dived steeply and

Heated tents are necessary to allow mechanics to work on engines in bitterly cold conditions

was probably destroyed. Sergeant-Pilot Drew, also on his first real engagement, got himself two MC 200s, one of which he saw hit the ground: "It was easy as breakfast in bed", he is recorded as saying. Pilot Officer Duke attacked an MC 200 which was seen to spin in and crash by Sergeant-Pilot Evans. He also attacked another Macchi at ground level from dead astern and it flew into the ground and burst into flames. This kill was shared by Sergeant-Pilot Reid of No 3 Squadron RAAF.

'The enemy's defence was to adopt a circle, and when evading, to dive down to ground level in rolls and vertical dives. Sergeant-Pilot Leu attacked a MC 200 which blew up, and another one which went into the ground. Sergeant-Pilot Simonsen certainly destroyed one M 200 which he saw spin into the ground, and probably

he damaged another MC 200 which was enveloped in a sheet of flame at 1,000 feet. Sergeant-Pilot Christie claimed two MC 200s destroyed and another damaged. His account was that he dived and gave one Macchi a heavy burst so that the aircraft climbed steeply, and then spiralled and crashed, bursting into flames. He dived on the second, which stalled, pouring out black smoke and going into a dive. He had a go at a third and probably damaged it, but without any visible result. Sergeant-Pilot Evans also attacked a MC 200 which dived away so steeply that it was doubtful whether it could have pulled out. Pilot Officer Bartle gave another MC 200 a good burst which sent it down out of control and damaged a Messerschmitt 109F which he chased all the way to Tmimi.

'No 3 Squadron in the meanwhile were all about to fall on the bombers when they saw six Messerschmitt 109s lurking about. They wheeled round in time and in the ensuing dogfight four of them were destroyed and another one damaged. They then concentrated on the bombers. By the end of the fight the remnants of the enemy formation had fled. Of the estimated total strength, at the beginning, of thirty-two enemy aircraft, twenty were claimed destroyed, two probably destroyed and ten damaged. Neither of the Kittyhawk squadrons lost an aircraft in what was the text-book example of a perfect interception; both top and extra cover being eliminated before the bombers were attacked.

'No 3 RAAF Squadron were particularly pleased with their success as a lot of their pilots were newcomers. 112 Squadron's share of this total was eleven-and-a-half destroyed, two probables and three damaged. In that fight the squadron fired seven thousand and sixty rounds.' (An average of 614 rounds per plane shot down.)

The most dangerous airman in North Africa was *Hauptmann* Hans-Joachim Marseille, the 'Eagle of Africa' who arrived in the spring of 1941 to fly Me 109s with JG 27. For a German from a military family (his father, an infantry general, was killed at Stalingrad) Marseille was an unusually flamboyant character, as were some of the other German aces. This Luftwaffe pilot was uncannily accurate in his shooting: he was unexcelled in judging deflection angles and his tidy-minded armourers who kept a score of rounds expended for each kill assessed the amount of ammunition used by Marseille to be only fifteen rounds for each kill on average. His staggering list of 158 victories was complete by 30th September 1942 when, at the age of twenty-two, his Messerschmitt either caught fire or began to leak fumes into the cockpit over the desert near Cairo. In bailing out his body hit the tailplane. On the first day of the month, Marseille had shot down seventeen planes, all of them fighters, – during three sorties in one day!

When handled by the best Allied fighter pilots, P-40s could be successful against every type of enemy fighter they encountered but when pilots like Marseille were about the Curtiss plane was shown up to be clumsily obsolescent. The first victim to the German ace on the day of his big score, 1st September, was a P-40, one of ten which attacked Stukas being escorted by Me 109s. Six Spitfires, acting as top cover to the P-40s dived down to engage the Messerschmitts south of El Imayid. Marseille waited for the Spitfires to approach and as they banked to curve around on to his tail he momentarily lowered his flaps to increase his own turning rate and slow his plane so that the Spitfires shot past, the last in line being hit by his cannon and machine gun fire. That fight then quickly broke up and both sides withdrew. On his second flight, before 1100 hours that morning, he was among the top cover flight for Stukas when they all ran into another bomber and fighter party, an Allied group of Blenheims protected by P-40s, and Marseille led his wingmen into an attack on eight P-40s intent on diving on the Stukas. When this interception was made with height advantage to the enemy, the P-40s formed a protective circle, the middle of which Marseille found to be an ideal position for deflection shooting, knocking down two P-40s before the circle broke up, three more as they scattered and his sixth in the action after a long chase and a climbing, turning, deflection shot.

Another group of unsuspecting pilots flying P-40s crossed beneath him over the desert soon afterwards and, unseen, Marseille approached alone to claim his seventh victim. Heading home he came upon a P-40 which had been hit in its glycol system; it was trailing white smoke and was probably the easiest target of the lot to shoot down. The score for his second flight of the morning was eight P-40s in ten minutes. When he landed he found *Feldmarschall* Kesselring at the Operations HQ. Informed that the squadron had shot down twelve enemy fighters that morning, Kesselring asked Marseille how many he had shot down, and Marseille had replied: 'Twelve, sir.' Kesselring is reported as being 'speechless'.

For airmen on both sides it was a busy day. The Battle of Alam Halfa had opened the night before with the German offensive beginning near El Hemeimat to advance towards the Alam Halfa ridge. Rommel was eventually forced to withdraw and the battle was inconclusive, although the New Zealand Division was confidently prepared to chase Rommel to the sea.

The troops could not always see the air force in action, carrying out helpful attacks against the enemy over his lines, and therefore without further consideration supposed the airmen to be having an easy time. Just a simple escorting flight to the port at Sidi Barrani or encampments

at Derna was a hazardous operation with people like Marseille about. In the evening of 1st September, he again took off on an escort flight, covering Ju 88s seeking to bomb British troop concentrations. Fifteen P-40s attacked the bombers over their target area and Marseille's pilots followed the attackers to begin a dogfight which raged for only six minutes, from 5,000 feet down to almost ground level. Marseille shot down five P-40s, bringing his day's total to seventeen! Not one of the fighters from his squadron had been shot down through all these actions and during the six days of the Battle of Alam Halfa they accounted for sixty-one Allied aircraft. The Luftwaffe pilots celebrated their aerial victories at a cocktail bar Marseille had installed in his desert tent.

During 1942 the numbers of Kittyhawks in the Desert increased until they were at least numerically superior to the enemy. Some Spitfires had been brought across from Malta for use as top cover fighters although, in most operations, Kittyhawks sent out on low-level strafing and bombing missions used the services of other Kittyhawks to protect them from German and Italian fighters. The four RAF, two RAAF and two SAAF Kittyhawk squadrons gave close support to the British Eighth Army in clashes with Rommel's *Afrika Korps* during that year. The decisive Battle of El Alamein was fought at the end of October and the Allies landed on the shores of French North Africa on the night of 7th/8th November.

Converting North African P-40s to bomb-carriers increased the destructive power of Montgomery's air support. Previously there had been very few experimental conversions of the type in any of its operating theatres. The American Volunteer Group in China, who did not receive their first few P-40Es until March 1942, by when the pilots were taking turns to fly the dozen or so remaining Tomahawks, were keen to add bombs to bullets.

The number of Japanese aircraft officially credited to the group was 286, eleven of the pilots scoring ten or more and the top man, Robert H Neale, destroying sixteen while flying P-40s. The group's early attempts to use their Hawks as fighter-bombers were not very successful, since they were handicapped by having no bomb-rack conversion kits; the 30-pound incendiary and fragmentation bombs they did drop were released from the flare chute positioned behind the cockpit in the fuselage.

The development of the fighter into a fighter-bomber was being worked out at about this time by engineers in the Desert Air Force. Clive Caldwell's 112 Squadron and the RAAF 3 Squadron began experiments with racks and release equipment produced by the versatile engineers in the RAF work-shops at Amriya. There was of course a well-established formula for such conversions but as each make of aircraft had its own peculiarities in reacting to external additions there was no guarantee that the bomb would fall free of the propeller.

Abandoned Fiat G-50 fighters on the field at Sidi Rezegh after its capture in January 1941

Caldwell chose to carry out the first test himself and in making the first run with the new racks he dropped an unfused 250-pound bomb and, in case it hit the propeller as it left the rack, he made the test run over the sea where a crashing aircraft would only kill fish. That test and his following test with a live bomb were both successful. After more testing, RAAF headquarters decided to form a fighter-bomber wing of Kittyhawks, 112 Squadron being the first squadron to convert. Pilots of conventional dive-bombers, such as the Dauntless and Stuka, were thoroughly trained in their system of aiming and dropping, whereas fighter pilots had to invent their own methods. The conventional dive-bomber could dive slowly at a steep angle, braked in the air by special flaps, and their wings were designed to provide high lift for the pull-out. P-40s could not dive close to the ground, their speed building up too

113

quickly, so they let their bombs go at a much higher altitude. The US fighter pilot arrived at a technique of diving at an angle of forty-five degrees, then, as he slowly made the pull-out, and when the target in the gunsight passed below and out of sight under the aircraft's nose, he counted, one for every one thousand feet of height above the target, until the plane was almost flying level, then released the bomb. With the use of delayed action bombs it was a simpler matter to fly low and let them loose about fifty feet from the target. Various systems were tried and with plenty of practice the fighter pilots became accurate bombadiers.

In May 1942, the month in which the Japanese received their first check, at the Battle of the Coral Sea in their drive on Port Moresby, Rommel was preparing for his third counter offensive in the Western Desert. On the 26th he struck, eventually forcing the British armour back, and at the same time sending a Panzer column against the flank at Bir Hakeim where the line was held by Free French forces. The entire Desert Air Force were sent out on continuous strikes against Rommel's tanks and transports. The wing comprising 3, 112 and 274 Squadrons averaged 350 sorties a day during the first four days. The fighter-bombers were in action on the morning of the 27th, Caldwell's squadron destroying nine and damaging thirty-eight vehicles in low-level attacks. The following day the pilots flew three to four sorties each to destroy another eighteen vehicles and damage twenty-two. These successes established the P-40 as a useful bomb-carrier, a role unplanned in the prewar designs for this type of aircraft. In future, P-40s were to be used mainly in close ground-support operations.

At Bir Hakeim the Free French fought desperately for sixteen days until ordered by General Ritchie to withdraw under cover of darkness on the night of 10th June. On 1st July the Germans reached El Alamein where the fighting stretched forty miles out to the Qattara Depression. Then the Germans withdrew to prepare for the Battle of Alam Halfa which took place at the end of August. It was only a few weeks after this point in the desert war that General Montgomery had his Eighth Army positioned for the dramatic climax of the Battle of El Alamein which opened on the night of 23rd October. Everything flyable was sent in by the Desert Air Force supporting the British and Common-wealth troops who routed the enemy after intense tank, gun, mortar, rifle and bayonet action. As the Germans retreated they filled the narrow road leading to the west with every kind of vehicle that could carry men and necessary equipment. If every fighter had been equipped to carry bombs and had been flown with the same skill and determination as the experienced Kittyhawk pilots, Rommel would have lost even the remnants of his *Korps* which, as it was, remained sufficiently strong to make formidable stands during the long retreat.

To give the P-40 a high-altitude performance not possible with the Allison engine, as it then lacked turbo-supercharging, a P-40D was fitted with a Rolls-Royce Merlin 28 and became prototype XP-40F. The results were so satisfying that Curtiss decided to build a production model using Rolls-Royce engines built under licence by Packard. Thus the P-40F was powered by the Packard Merlin V-1650-1, rated at 1,300hp for take-off and 1,102hp at 18,500 feet. With a three-blade airscrew and weighing 8,500 pounds, the P-40F reached its top speed of 364mph at 20,000 feet and had a service ceiling of 34,400 feet.

Although ordered by the RAF and designated Kittyhawk II, no P-40Fs were received into that service, the production going instead to the Soviet Union, the Free French and the USAAF. Americans flew them into action, with USAAF Spitfires, during the invasion of French North Africa. In this operation squadrons of

USAAF P-40s flew for the first time off aircraft-carriers which carried them close to the Tunisian coast.

Endeavouring to increase the performance of the Merlin-engined P-40, Curtiss produced 700 in a stripped version the P-40L, known as 'Gipsy Rose Lee' Warhawks, with only four guns and less armour and fuel, but their top speed was only a few miles per hour faster than the heavier type. Because of a shortage of Packard Merlins in North Africa, some of the P-40Fs were refitted with Allisons when their original motors wore out. Engines used in the re-engined P-40Ls were the same as those used in the P-40Ms.

The next production model to go into service with the British and Commonwealth air forces was the Kittyhawk III, a designation which covered both P-40Ks and P-40Ms. The more powerful Allison V-1710-73 engine used in the P-40K was more efficient than previous types, having an automatic pressure regulator and rotary valve cooling. It produced 1,325hp for take-off and 1,150hp at 11,800 feet. During take-off the early model P-40Ks tended to swing harder than normally and a dorsal fin strake was fitted to try to counteract this; later models compensated the torque swing with a slight lengthening of the fuselage.

For its destined role as a fighter-bomber, the P-40K's performance was adequate in late 1942: maximum speeds of 320mph at 5,000 feet and 362mph at 15,000 feet, and a cruising speed of 290mph. Its empty weight was 6,400 pounds, maximum was up to 10,000 pounds. Although the RAF received only twenty-one P-40Ks, 1,300 were built, serving in the Chinese air force and with USAAF forces in the Pacific and Asia. Top scorer in Warhawks was David 'Tex' Hill, a colonel in the USAAF, who shot down eighteen Japanese aircraft.

P-40Ms were fitted with Allison V-1710-81 engines which gave an almost uniform horse-power from take-off (1,200hp) to 14,600 feet (1,125 hp) and an emergency power of 1,360hp for combat. Maximum speed was 360 mph, cruising speed 272mph and, while its empty weight was only eighty pounds greater than that of the K model, it was restricted to a maximum loaded weight of 8,900 pounds. With auxiliary fuel its range was 1,600 miles and its service ceiling was 30,000 feet. While Curtiss had made some construction progress on their projected P-60 design, the demand for fighters was so immediate that P-40 production continued instead and hundreds more were rolled out from the factories. British and Commonwealth air forces received 600 P-40Ms and 1,300 P-40Ks were built.

The severest climatic conditions under which P-40s operated were found in the Aleutians and Alaska where freezing conditions not only restricted flying operations but maintenance as well. In the depths of winter, with the temperature gauges constantly below freezing point, the engines were kept covered with canvas and unfrozen with the use of oil heaters. America manned two forts in the string of Aleutians that extended out from Alaska, defining the limits of the Pacific and the Bering Sea. The main base, Dutch Harbour, was on Unalaska Island, 140 miles out from the mainland. The Japanese feared American advances from this spear of islands, which pointed in the direction of the Japanese home islands, and they landed on Kiska and Attu to establish outpost observation and reconnaissance stations after a raid launched from carriers on 3rd/4th June 1942. The sky all the year round was consistently overcast, a clear day was a rare occurrence and gusty winds often blew from the Siberian land mass. 'Williwaw' hurricanes and fog and mist prevented any flights on numerous occasions.

After the Japanese occupation of the two outlying islands America naturally expected an invasion of Dutch Harbour, although the Japa-

nese had made no plans for anything but the observation posts, where airfields were constructed. The US retaliated with strikes against Kiska and Attu and, in August, US troops moved to Adak unopposed to get closer to the enemy. P-40s and P-39s patrolled without interference while a strip was constructed on Adak Island. Both Canadian and US P-40s joined the bomber flow attacking supplies and communications on Kiska. The Japanese maintained few aircraft there, relying mainly on float-planes for reconnaissances. On 25th September the Kittyhawks destroyed two Nakajima A6M2-N Rufes and about eight float biplanes on the water while the bombers scored a direct hit on a transport.

Amchitka Island was occupied by US forces and from the new strip constructed there they made strafing raids as the 11th Air Force built up for the operations designed to clear the enemy from the Aleutians. During two weeks in April an average of sixty aircraft per day were over Kiska, the

Kitty-bomber of the famous Shark Squadron takes off in a cloud of dust with its 250lb bomb

fighters contributing the most effective bombing as they could manoeuvre under the clouds better than the bombers and therefore strike more accurately. The P-40s carried a 500-pound bomb under the belly and six 20-pound fragmentation or incendiary bombs under the wings, using glide-bombing tactics when it was impossible to dive-bomb and following the drop with strafing runs against radar, hangars, aircraft and camps. In this period only one P-40 was lost to anti-aircraft fire and no air opposition was encountered.

Very bad weather delayed the Attu D-Day from 7th to 8th May when the US Army landed, covered and supported by eighty P-40s, twenty-six P-39s, and sixty-two bombers, the old K and M model P-40s doing most of the work. Japanese air reaction first appeared on 22nd May, when twelve or more bombers came in out of the murk and ineffectively raided the US strips. When the bombers returned two days later P-39s shot down five. The Attu defence ended after a fanatical counter attack by hundreds of screaming Japanese, who died in the attempt. That was on the second last day of May 1943 and the Kiska invasion was planned for 15th August, the day the Kittyhawk squadrons of the 407th Bombardment Group (Dive) were redesignated the 407th Fighter-Bomber Group.

The fighter-bombers continued to give valuable assistance in softening up Kiska until D-Day, which was delayed because of 'williwaws' and other dreadful acts of nature, and abandoned again on D plus 1. On D plus 2 an observer flying over the island saw no sign of any movement at all, and decided correctly that the Japanese had evacuated. The evacuation order had been issued by Vice-Admiral Tetuo Akiyama on 8th June and successfully carried out under the cover of cloud, rain and fog. During these operations the stolid P-40 proved that it could operate in the freeze as well as in the Desert and the humid conditions of the SWPA.

Knocking out targets in awkwardly situated positions required the use of more agile aircraft than light and medium bombers, especially if the target was small and bad weather interfered with bomb-aimers' vision. Such targets called for fighter-bombers to weave up to a pin-point at relatively low level, fast enough to be missed by much of the anti-aircraft fire. The US 51st Group in Burma demonstrated how P-40s could fill this role successfully when they destroyed bridges on the main Japanese supply line to Myitkyina. In April 1943, before the monsoons arrived to slow down aerial and rail activity, P-40s took over from B-25s in the vital bridge-busting missions, also taking over the B-25s 1,000-pound bombs which, as Lieutenant-Colonel J E Barr demonstrated to the Group, could be lifted by the Kittyhawks.

Wending their way through the rough country, the fighter-bombers destroyed several bridges, and when the Japanese repaired them the Americans blew them up again, severely restricting rail traffic until in May the rains came, and adding to the enemy's supply difficulties.

When the monsoon season ended the Tenth Air Force replaced the K and M model P-40s with the N model, P-51As and P-38s. The 1,000-pounders were dropped by P-40s on the Myitkyina airfield, variously-fused bombs that left large crater scars across the field rendering it temporarily unserviceable; when the holes had been filled, repeat raids by P-40s with the big bombs excavated more.

In China, the 80th Fighter Group operating with the Fourteenth Air Force were equipped with P-40Ns and they too carried 1,000-pound bombs in attacks on major targets. Planes from this group flew fighter-bomber missions into Indo-China in March 1944, unopposed while they attacked supply bases and rail and river transport. On one raid the P-40s really extended their range ambitions, flying down to Hanoi in an attempt to flood the Gia Lam aerodrome by breaching the dikes. The twenty-two P-40s, escorted by two P-38s which also carried bombs, made a breach and the water flowed out, too low, however, to make a worthwhile flood. On the way back eight of the P-40s ran out of fuel, two force-landing and six being abandoned in the air, one pilot being killed.

On one occasion in the war in eastern China a flight of P-40s was attacked with the tactics that P-40s considered their own: a flight of Japanese fighters dived down and instead of staying down at the P-40s' height and mixing in a dogfight, where the Zeros would have anyway been superior, they made their passes and pulled up again to ready for another dive. Using these manoeuvres they shot down three P-40s for the loss of two Zeros.

Yamamoto's I-Go Sakusen

Early in 1943, USAAF units in the SWPA were being re-equipped with P-38 Lightnings while the RAAF re-equipped with Spitfires, for the North-Western defences, and Kittyhawk IIIs for new formations of fighter squadrons. By the end of 1943 the RAAF had received 485 P-40s. As well as 75 and 76 Squadrons, there were 77, 78, 80, 82 and 86 Squadrons formed or in process of forming to operate the fighter-bombers on escort, defence, strafing and bombing missions, attacking a variety of targets in areas around New Britain and along the New Guinea coast, and later, when the Rabaul base was virtually surrounded and sealed off, supporting advancing Allied troops as they progressed to the Halmaheras. A great percentage of the operations involved long flights over the sea, requiring more careful maintenance to keep the single engine in reliable condition, and a large air-sea rescue force of flying-boats and surface vessels.

During 1942, the Japanese air forces stationed around the southern edge of the Greater East Asia Co-prosperity Sphere, were drastically whittled down in interceptions and airfield attacks in the Darwin, New Guinea and Solomons areas, by anti-aircraft guns and by fighters flown from US aircraft-carriers. As late as August the Japanese continued to send bombers over Darwin on daylight raids which were proving very costly to them. In one raid, on the 23rd, Kittyhawks of the US 49th Group shot down eight fighters and four bombers, damaging many others which would not have made their bases. When the Japanese changed to night bombing their raids were mostly ineffectual and provided good night-fighting practice for the two RAAF squadrons which relieved the 49th Group. Daylight raids continued over Darwin into

Fleet Admiral Isoroku Yamamoto, Commander-in-Chief of the Japanese fleet until his death

1943, when Spitfires were defending the base.

At Milne Bay, Turnbull Strip had been completed and 75 Squadron, commanded by Squadron Leader W S Arthur DSO, DFC, another veteran from 3 Squadron, returned to operate from the base early in 1943. Arthur carried out the first test of a Kittyhawk carrying a 1,000-pound bomb and four 40-pound bombs, with full complement of ammunition and fuel. This had not been attempted in the SWPA before; unfortunately he had to return with the load intact since his target at Gasmata was too thickly covered with cloud. After being stationed in West Australia, 76 Squadron too returned to the Pacific, based at Goodenough Island, and formed a wing with 75. The squadron was now commanded by Squadron Leader Ian Loudon who joined 76 Squadron as a sergeant-pilot in 1942. 77 Squadron also flew into Milne Bay to complete the Kittyhawk wing, but the squadrons were continually moved about in their work of helping to close the noose around Rabaul. The squadrons were all equipped with P-40K Kittyhawk IIIs.

At this time the Japanese air forces were composed of the Fourth Air Army, made up of two divisions, and the Navy's XI Air Fleet, made up of two air flotillas. Their aircraft were on bases radiating from Rabaul to New Guinea and the North Solomons. By March, the morale of Japanese air crews had fallen very low. The most important reason for this was the high loss of aircraft in the Rabaul area – including Lae-Port Moresby – and other important factors contributing to the degeneration of morale were the superiority in number and the quality of newer Allied fighter aircraft, particularly Lightnings and Beaufighters, and the breaking down of the aircraft supply system between Japan and her southern bases. Of all the Japanese military leaders, Yamamoto at least could have been expected to see the

writing on the wall after the Bismarck Sea disaster. But he seemed to have been out of touch and misled by his staff who accepted inaccurate reports of losses.

Yamamoto had assumed personal command of the air forces in the area, establishing his headquarters at Rabaul, and made plans for retaliatory attacks which would, he hoped, reduce Allied superiority in the air. Beginning on 7th April, he launched his Operation-A, *I-Go Sakusen*, using all his available aircraft in a series of fighter and bomber attacks on Allied shipping and aircraft bases in New Guinea and the Solomons. The plan would have been realistic enough, if he had had his old aircrews. But his forces were weakened by inexperienced reinforcements, some of them naval pilots with only thirty hours carrier training, and the lack of bombing and fighting skill could not be compensated by numbers of aircraft. Too many of his accurate and skilful

airmen, from the Nagumo task force and from the Lae Wing, had been shot down, killed in accidents or drowned, whereas the Allies were stronger in air crews that had been reinforced with experienced men and others who had been given a sound training.

American ships at anchor off the Guadalcanal coast, ships in Oro Bay, and the air bases at Port Moresby and Milne Bay were attacked. Some shipping was sunk and some planes were shot-up or shot down, but the results were nothing like the claims made by the Japanese airmen.

77 Squadron claimed its first daylight 'kill' on the 11th, when twelve of their Kittyhawks were scrambled to intercept bombers and fighters at 25,000 feet, a long way up for the slow-climbing Kittyhawks. Two intercepted, claiming one Zero shot down and one probable. When Port Moresby was raided on the 12th, a mixture of Allied fighters – Lightnings, P-39s and Beaufighters – shot down twenty-four

Japanese planes for the loss of two fighters in the air, a Beaufighter and three B-25s destroyed and fifteen assorted aircraft damaged on the ground. Runways were also damaged and some men were killed near an exploding fuel dump. At Oro Bay on the same day a large raid was made on Allied shipping in which a 2,000-ton cargo ship received two direct hits and a smaller supply ship and a corvette were damaged. For this loss at least seventeen Japanese aircraft were shot down by P-40s and Lightnings. In a raid on Milne Bay two days later Japanese success with about one hundred aircraft was limited to a few men wounded and the runway cratered. Seventeen of 75 Squadron's Kittyhawks, all that were serviceable, scrambled to the interception, shooting down two bombers, two Zeros and one dive-bomber without loss to themselves.

The Japanese claimed that they had shot down 134 Allied aircraft and mini-

Troops and supplies are dropped in the campaign to drive the Japanese from Lae

mised their own losses to forty-nine. They also claimed that they had destroyed many more Allied aircraft at bases which they claimed were also severely damaged, and that they had sunk a cruiser, two destroyers and twenty-five cargo and transport ships. These false claims persuaded Yamamoto to believe that *I-Go Sakusen* had succeeded and he released what was left of the 1 Carrier Division's aircraft for other duties.

To make a personal assessment of his 'victory' and to discuss future operations with General Hyakutake, commander of the Seventeenth Army in the Solomons, Yamamoto planned to fly down from Rabaul to Bougainville on 18th April. His visit to the front lines was to be made with meticulous timing of departures and arrivals; the admiral was very strict on

121

punctuality. One radio signal and adherence to the exact flight plan contributed to the loss of Japan's naval genius.

American cipher experts had broken the Japanese navy's code, and one idle piece of chatter announcing Yamamoto's forthcoming journey, despite the strictest ruling that his movements were top secret and not to be mentioned in radio communication, was picked up and quickly sent to US Navy Headquarters at Pearl Harbor

Japanese G4 ML bomber. Yamamoto was travelling in a 'Betty' when it was intercepted and destroyed; he was thrown out and killed

for decoding. Yamamoto's ability was considered by the Allies to be so valuable to the Japanese in their strategic planning and tactical operations that he headed the high priority list of enemy leaders to be killed or captured at the earliest opportunity. At last an opportunity had arisen.

The knowledge that he would be almost within the range of Army fighters produced a flurry of messages between Washington, Pearl Harbor and Major John W Mitchell, P-38 Lightning squadron commander at Henderson Field, Guadalcanal. It was known that two Betty bombers, one carrying Yamamoto and staff officers,

the other carrying another admiral, Kitamura, and other staff officers, escorted by six Zeros, would take off from Rabaul at 0600hrs. It was just possible to make interception close to the known destination and 430 miles from Henderson Field. To increase the Lightnings' normal range, special drop tanks were hurriedly flown out. On the morning of the interception, two of Mitchell's eighteen fighters returned to base with engine trouble and the others intercepted, four concentrating on the two Betty bombers while twelve flew cover against the Zeros. Lieutenant Lanphier dived his Lightning onto the tail of the leading Betty, Yamamoto's aircraft, firing a long burst from his cannon and machine guns and setting alight the starboard wing, which broke off. The bomber crashed into the jungle. The second Betty was also hit by Lightnings as it tried to escape by flying low over the jungle, and crashed into the sea. Three Zeros were also shot down. Only one Lightning was lost. Kitamura, Vice-Admiral Ugaki and the pilot of the ditched bomber were the only survivors from the second Betty. Yamamoto's body, still strapped in the co-pilot's seat and with a sword in his hand, was thrown clear of the wreckage. It was left to Kitamura and Ugaki to realize what a failure Operation-A had been.

Kiwis in Kittyhawks

During the few weeks of vague aftermath following the Japanese thrust into the Pacific, when the extent of their objectives was still unknown and any country along the vast spread of the Ocean could expect to suddenly find enemy transports steaming towards its shores, New Zealand too sent out a call to Britain and America for fighters. New Zealand's defences were not strong at that time. The nucleus of manpower consisted of a few experienced army men who had fought with their famed division in the Middle East and some aircrew who had served with the RAF. At this time of crisis, more airmen were recalled to their homeland. The quality of the fighter pilots can be gauged from the proportionately strong representation of New Zealanders in Battle of Britain squadrons. The first New Zealand ace was 'Cobber' Kain who had seventeen certain victories flying Hurricanes in France before its fall. Al Deere won his spurs in Spitfires during the Battle, and the famous leader of 11 Group, Keith Park, was a New Zealander. On average, no better airmen flew either in single or multi-engined aircraft during the war.

There were, in December 1941, no modern fighter aircraft in New Zealand. The country lay too far south for any but carrier-borne aircraft to attack her cities and bases, in which event the US Navy would be expected to intervene. In any case a Japanese involvement in the war was not really expected. The nearest Pacific islands were Fiji and New Caledonia, hundreds of miles to the north; north again from these lay the Solomon Islands. To maintain vigilance over the sea approaches were thirty-six Hudsons and thirty-five Vincents. Apart from trainers, the rest of the Royal New Zealand Air Force's aircraft were obsolete. The country had not been used by the US as a stage on the delivery route to the NEI so there were no passing Allied aircraft, as there were at Darwin, to divert for immediate defence. The appeal for fighters to

the UK was successful, or partly so, for the British Government released 142 Kittyhawks destined for the Middle East to Australia and New Zealand, and by the end of April 1942, eighteen had arrived in the 'Shaky Isles'. An extra eighty were allocated but by July only another forty-four had been delivered.

Using the first batch of eighteen P-40s, K and M models, a new squadron, 14, was quickly formed in April 1942. 15 and 16 formed in June with the further deliveries of Ks and Ms and 17 formed in October. Fortunately, during these slow deliveries in 1942, the Japanese did not consider marauding with aircraft-carriers into the southern seas. In the following year and in 1944 three other Kittyhawk squadrons, 18, 19 and 20 were formed. All of the squadrons later changed their P-40s for Corsairs during 1944 when other new squadrons were also formed and equipped with Corsairs. By then, however, the Japanese had been swept from the south west Pacific skies, many falling to the guns of P-40s.

With its growing reserve of pilots, some returned from the Middle East and European theatres, others coming up in large batches from the Empire Air Training schools, the RNZAF planned short tours in the Pacific for the squadrons, ensuring a high standard of training between tours and giving the pilots a better chance to maintain their physical fitness. The rotation planned for fighter squadrons was six weeks in a combat area, three weeks in support and nine weeks in New Zealand. The system reduced the necessity for training large groups of replacements to the fighting standards reached by those who would have experienced one or two tours. Some men in the new squadrons had been bomber pilots who chose to convert to fighters.

The ubiquitous Hudsons were the first of New Zealand's air force to operate against the Japanese, flying patrols and reconnaissances from the islands in the north, and it was not until April 1943 that RNZAF fighters joined their American allies in the fighting zone of Guadalcanal. The previous year 14 Squadron had been based at Santo and 15 had taken over twenty-three neglected P-40s of the US 68th Pursuit Squadron on Tonga. These aircraft had no engine spare parts – the USAAF's practice at the time was to send whole engines back to the United States for reconditioning – and most of the gun barrels were badly eroded. Fortunately, there was no call to combat in these areas. At Guadalcanal, where costly battles had been fought for the possession of Henderson airfield, the Japanese were supplied and reinforced from the Rabaul base, 675 miles away. The Japanese had lost the fight for Henderson after their major attempt to land reinforcements by sea was defeated at the Battle of Guadalcanal – the third great turning point of the Pacific war. The fighting nevertheless continued in the Solomons and on 6th May RNZAF Kittyhawks were in action. Two of them escorting a Hudson shot down a floatplane. Two days later 15 Squadron joined an Allied air attack on three Japanese destroyers that had run into a minefield which left one crippled and one

The rainy season on Guadalcanal makes life difficult even without the Japanese

aground. Landing craft were also attacked as they attempted to land survivors.

In their first engagement with Japanese fighters, the Kiwis shot down four without loss, although two P-40s were forced to crash-land on the Russell Island airstrip. Flight Sergeant Bob Martin was awarded a US Air Medal for the first Zero brought down by a New Zealander in the Pacific War. In this action twelve Kittyhawks were part of a force of forty-four Allied fighters which made contact with between forty and fifty Japanese fighters near the Russells and Buraku Island. In clouded and squally skies, the resulting dogfight continued for an hour and a half, the Allies claiming twenty-three for the loss of seven. In this action the Kiwis learned at first hand the amazing performance of the Zero. Flying Officer G H Owen described in his report an interception of five Zeros by five Kittyhawks. The latter were climbing into the sun with two Zeros ('Zekes' in the report) on their tails, and then a dogfight ensued:

'Squadron Leader Herrick and Davis had joined us by this time, making a total of five P-40s against five Zekes. We made several attacks and passes, more or less individually. McKenzie and my leader then dropped out with gun trouble, and Martin had also dropped out. I saw two Zekes on Davis's tail – the first one firing all guns, with the second Zeke above and slightly in the rear, not firing, but protecting the first Zeke. I made a left hand turn and fired a long full deflection burst into the leading Zeke. As I turned with the attack I saw another Zeke about a thousand feet below me and flying level – I did not pay attention to this plane as I did not think it possible for it to join the fight, but as I was firing at the Zeke on Davis's tail I noticed tracers coming up past the fuselage, and my plane was hit. I looked down and saw this lower Zeke firing at a distance of only 60-70 yards away.'

This was an excellent example of the

Above : Acting Wing Commander Trevor Owen Freeman DSO DFC
Right : Squadron Leader Cresswell displays the international flags on his Kittyhawk based on Vivigani strip

high rate of climb advantage possessed by the Zero, although its speed, when first sighted by Owen, could have been much higher than in normal level flight if it had just come out of a dive. Its momentum would have carried it up to the P-40 more quickly than a normal climb could have done.

On 12th June, one of Yamamoto's big fighter sweeps sent out to destroy the Allied air bases was intercepted north and north east of the Russells. 14 Squadron had arrived the previous day to relieve 15, and eight of the new arrivals were part of the force of ninety Allied fighters intercepting. One New Zealander was lost in the engagement, during which the eight New Zealanders shot down six Japanese, a large share of the total of twenty-five Zeros downed. The third and largest Japanese attack in this month of massive retaliation took place four days later. More than a hundred dive-bombers and fighters flew over, searching for ground and sea targets. Control scrambled 10 Allied fighters, seventy-four of which made contact with the enemy. It wa

a disaster for the Japanese who lost eighty-eight aircraft, eleven to anti-aircraft fire and the rest to intercepting Wildcats and P-40s. The Allies lost only six aircraft and the New Zealanders, who shot down five Japanese, lost none. Some of the dive-bombers got through to sink a cargo ship and one LST. In attempting to stop the Allied progression towards the base at Rabaul, the Japanese had lost 160 aircraft in a short space of time. Compared with the Allies' loss of twenty-nine, the Japanese losses were a major blow to their hopes of holding on in the SWPA.

Altogether there were eleven major air attacks launched by the Japanese during this period, the last being made on 15th July. The cost was too high to continue with the losses the Japanese were sustaining, brought about mainly by the poor quality of reinforcement Japanese pilots and the vulnerability of the planes to .50-inch bullets, heavy enough to explode or disintegrate the light, poorly armoured Zeros. Sergeant (later Squadron Leader) Nairn demonstrated on 3rd July, when 14 Squadron shot down five without loss, how the less manoeuvrable Kittyhawk could survive in a dogfight with Zeros by using aggressive tactics, working desperately hard and having a little luck.

Nairn reported: 'I concentrated on the nearest of these Zekes and put a good burst into him. I could see smoke from incendiaries coming from him, but he flew away and I did not see him again, being myself attacked by six aircraft from the starboard quarter, and by others from astern. I again took the same evasive action.

'I left these aircraft to mill around by themselves and I saw two Zekes in close formation ahead of me. I overtook them and put a long burst, dead astern, into the leader. As I was firing, at about 150 yards, I was attacked by a number of Zekes from beam and astern, and my aircraft was hit by a cannon shell in the port wing, and by sundry bullets. White petrol vapour trails came from the fuselage or wing root of the Zeke I had attacked. He rolled on his back, and pulled out under and to starboard of me. The white smoke turned to heavy black smoke. I was busy evading his mates by a violent downward skid to the right I was then at 6,000 to 7,000 feet. As I came out of this manoeuvre, I saw a circular white patch of foam on the water some 4,000 to 5,000 feet below me. There was also oil around the splash area. There was no further sign of this enemy aircraft, which I claim as destroyed.

'Six enemy aircraft, which had followed me down, were joined by possibly another ten. They came in from astern, above and both sides, entirely boxing me in, except from below. I could see tracer going past me. I turned toward the nearest aircraft and fired at them. I passed very close, about one foot from the nearest Zeke. My aircraft was faster at this level, and I broke out, but they followed me and I turned back into them to find that about three were supporting one Zeke, which made a head-on attack. Others were higher. I fired at the attacker and broke away down to avoid a head-on collision. This aircraft, I consider, tried to ram. The Zekes then appeared to give up the fight, as they merely sat above me and did not attack.

'After another encounter with other Zekes, I saw further aircraft which I thought might be Allied aircraft, so I went to join them, but found they were all Zekes. I attacked the nearest and put a good burst into him from the quarter until finally only one gun of my aircraft was firing. I then broke away and dived to sea level, and came home at about 5,000 feet with my aircraft damaged.'

Nairn decided that determined action was enough to upset these Japanese, making them sheer of

Pattern of bombs clusters around Japanese shipping in Rabaul Harbour, 12th August 1942

from attempts to swing from head-on or side-on approaches around to his tail. It is possible that when one tried to ram him, the Zeros in that group were out of ammunition.

The first two Kittyhawk squadrons formed saw most of the fighter action. When 16 took over from 14 on 25th July the big dogfighting period had ended and the relieving squadron was mostly engaged in bomber escort and in maintaining patrols, the same duties falling to 17 when they relieved 16 on 15th September. In October, the RNZAF increased its fighter squadron representation by sending up a two-squadron wing, composed of 15 and 18 Squadrons, to New Georgia where it operated with USAAF and USMC squadrons, supporting the Bougainville lan-

Corsairs, effective and sturdy fighter planes. Unlike P-40s, they could operate from carriers

dings early in November. The wing leader was Wing Commander T O Freeman DSO, DFC, RAF. When he was later shot down by Zeros during a raid on Rabaul he was replaced by Wing Commander C W K Nicholls DSO, RAF.

Eight Kittyhawks from 18 intercepted a group of from fifty to sixty Zeros inland while the Bougainville landing operations were taking place, shooting down seven and one probable in the space of a few minutes for the loss of one Kittyhawk. The pilot of this plane, Flying Officer K D Lumsden, was very lucky to survive a remarkable series of attacks from friend and enemy alike. First he was attacked by two Zeros near the landing area and had successfully extricated himself from their fire when he was fired on by a US destroyer whose shooting holed his aircraft. Then he was attacked by a Corsair fighter and shortly afterwards

was forced to ditch. Finally a barge appeared, its crew firing machine guns wildly and inaccurately at him before deciding that he might be on their side and plucking him from the water, unscathed.

RNZAF P-40s first carried bombs on operations on 11th December. Three of them, each carrying two 100-pound bombs, demolished buildings at Kietat with direct hits. Three days later the bomb-carriers were again successful, destroying a bridge in south west Bougainville. Such accuracy in early attempts on operations said much for the sound instruction passed on to the pilots by fighter bomb-droppers from Europe.

The Kittyhawks flew from Odonga, staging through Torokina to join Allied fighter swarms sweeping over Rabaul. The New Zealand squadrons managed to find action in an elaborate dogfight that extended from 18,000

feet down to sea-level. Accompanied by twenty-four US fighters, the Kitty-hawks were intercepted by more than forty Zeros. The New Zealanders lost five but their share of the destruction to the enemy was twelve shot down, four probables and several damaged. In the first 'charge', the P-40s chased a group of Zeros straight through another Japanese group and every New Zealand pilot made contact with a Zero during the fight. This was their last big action. With the decimation of the Japanese air force in this area taking place so rapidly, opportunities for interception were rare. The New Zealanders were engaged only six times in the last ten days of January 1944, shooting down eight Zeros for the loss of three P-40s. Their duties were mainly base patrol, sweep, escort and armed reconnaissance.

The final engagement for RNZAF Kittyhawks, or any of their fighters, was when twenty-five Zeros attacked 18 Squadron flying escort to US bombers raiding Vunakanau airfield. One P-40 was lost and two Zeros were shot down. These two Zeros brought the RNZAF Pacific score of Japanese aircraft shot down to ninety-nine, nearly all of them fighters. From then on, it was fighter-bombing and strafing for the New Zealanders, as it was at this time for the RAAF P-40s. The Kiwis also carried 500-pounders – incendiary, general purpose, incendiary clusters – or a belly tank of petrol-oil-incendiary. Occasionally they carried the large 1,000-pounders. By the end of all their Pacific operations the RNZAF had destroyed 200 barges and small craft.

During 1944, faster and more powerful Corsair fighters, with a better range for the long oversea flights, replaced the Kittyhawks and the New Zealand fighter squadrons continued to fly fighter-bomber missions and patrols throughout the various Allied operations which eventually led to the encirclement and cutting off of the Japanese Rabaul base.

Kittyhawk IV

In 1943 the fortunes of war were increasingly better for the Allies while all the Axis ground, sea and air forces were hard pressed whenever they were brought to action. Early in the year the siege of Leningrad was lifted, the German army at Stalingrad capitulated and the Japanese felt the power of Allied air strength in the Bismarck Sea. By the middle of the year the British Eighth Army had completed its work in North Africa, moving on with the US Seventh Army to land in Sicily, supported by a large air armada that included close-support Kittyhawks, on 9th July.

British and American fighters were vastly improved for operating with the armies, which had come to depend on them for an increasing variety of support. Army support developed into something much more complex than the old concept of army co-operation work and it was necessary to group together specialised sections for reconnaissance, strafing and dive-bombing ahead of the troops, destroying bridges and blocking roads, attacking tanks, vehicles, guns, small ships and trains and generally disrupting communications immediately behind the enemy's front. The first formation of a Tactical Air Force group was created in Britain on 14th June, and TAF squadrons operated in Italy when it was invaded on 3rd September by the Eighth Army, followed six days later by the US Fifth Army.

Bomb-carrying Kittyhawks were an important part of the TAF in Italy, where they flew on missions under the cover of Spitfires and Mustangs. The method now used for dropping bombs, apart from low-level bombing, is recorded in RAF P-40 squadron histories:

'The strike by the squadron usually followed a recce of the target by a Tac-R (tactical reconnaissance) Spitfire, and for strikes the aircraft were usually armed with two 250-pound bombs, fused either for instantaneous

First Allied aircraft to land on Kamiri strip, Noemfoor Island

or surface bursts. The earlier version of surface bomb used to have a long metal striker protruding out of the nose, which exploded the bomb above ground, thus not cratering. Later versions used in Sicily and Italy had pressure fuses, activated by the build-up of air pressure between the bomb and the ground. Anti-personnel bombs were carried beneath the wings. MT (Motor Transports – trucks etc.) were bombed in the following fashion; the leader, having spotted his target from a cruising altitude, manoeuvred his formation to cross the road at right angles, with his target inboard of his wing tip, and his section in echelon away from the target in loose formation. On a 'line' target, the main errors were 'short' or 'over' rather than lateral ones.

Chennault with Chinese officials

'The aircraft dived at a 60 degree angle from about 6,000 feet or 8,000 feet, down to 2,000 feet or 1,500 feet. With the target under his wing, and having told his section to arm their bombs, the leader would radio "Going down left (or right) now!" and would then wing-over into a diving turn. Using his reflector sight he would steady his aircraft on the target and start to pull out at about 2,500 feet, counting to ten and then releasing his bomb. The section bombed individually from line astern.

'The Kittyhawk was designed as a fighter aircraft and there was an element of luck, as well as skill, when it was being used as a bomber. Much depended on the leader, and where he put his section prior to the dive. If the dive was too steep the Kittyhawk would build up too much speed and would start to twist or roll, which

involved corrections and the aircraft would be skidded, which would throw the bomb sideways.'

After two years of fighter-bomber operations the aiming and dropping technique was still as primitive as ever but the loads the Kittyhawks dropped were more effectively lethal.

The next production model, the series P-40N-1-CU to P-40N-40-CU, known in the RAF as the Kittyhawk IV, included the slowest and fastest production P-40s. The fastest was the P-40N-1-CU which had its weight reduced by the removal of two guns, the fitting of lighter wheels and the use of lighter metals in various parts of its structure. This model, 400 of which were built, attained 378mph at 10,500 feet. The N-20 to N-35 series, of which 3,022 were built, had the two guns and full armour restored, yet were, at 6,000 pounds empty, the

lightest of the P-40 types and were able to carry the heaviest loads – to give them a loaded weight of 11,400 pounds. Some P-40Ns were converted to tandem two-seat trainers and others were modified for winter operations – that is, operations in the Canadian and Alaskan winters. In the P-40N-5-CU, the hood design was altered and increased glazing to the rear cockpit area improved the pilot's vision over his shoulder. A frameless sliding canopy replaced the older type which was divided into three panels.

As it was used as a fighter-bomber, the P-40N did not require the 400mph speed capability of its contemporaries. By 1944 it was such a full-time bomb-carrier in Europe that pilots were calling it the B-40. The 'bomber' pilots preferred to use their machines for aerial combat but duty forced them to accept what they considered a worse enemy than the Me 109s and Fw 190s – concentrated anti-aircraft fire. Losses to anti-aircraft fire were very heavy in Italy where it was rare to meet German fighters in any great number. When this did happen, the P-40s left them to the escorting Spitfires or Mustangs. In one fight over Rieti, a squadron of Kittyhawks had the advantage over a squadron of Fw 190s caught taking off from an airfield, the RAF pilots shooting down three and damaging three more for the loss of two of their own planes. Three 500-pound bombs was the normal load, but on short bombing missions in the TAF the fighters often carried a load approximating to that of the medium bombers of 1940, lifting a 1,000-pounder under the belly and two 500-pounders under the wings.

A contributing factor to Allied success in the SWPA air war was the enlistment of experienced road-building engineers and their construction equipment, loaders and dumpers, graders and bulldozers, that could build a strip in a matter of days. US Army Engineers and US Navy Seabees were lavishly equipped with earth-moving equipment whereas the Jap-

anese had practically none, relying on the use of captured airfields and using pick, shovel and muscle power to hack out the small fields and strips on outlying bases. As the Allies moved forward, their road and airstrip building equipment moved with them, going into operation as soon as the last snipers had been cleared away. A gravel mixing unit later built on Iwo Jima for B-29 airstrips would have satisfied the road-surfacing needs of a large town.

As Japanese forces a long way from the Home Islands came under pressure from Allied aircraft, the weakness of the long lines of communication left them dangerously exposed. Sung to the tune of 'John Peel', this composition by a Burma critic was very much to the point:
'Japs on the hilltop,
Japs in the chaung,
Japs on the Ngakyedauk,
Japs in the taung,
Japs with their L of C far too long,
As they revel in the joys of infiltration'.

In Burma, China and the Pacific areas, Allied forces were becoming too strong, as they extended their advance, for Japan to counter. As the Allies advanced through the islands and along the northern New Guinea coast, shipping, airfields, supply dumps and forts were attacked in non-stop operations, increasing in size every month and scoring on the Japanese with every sortie. MacArthur chose the Japanese-held Admiralty Islands as his jumping-off base for the invasion of the Philippines. US Cavalry units were sent in, with Kittyhawks of 76 and 77 Squadrons and Spitfires of 79 Squadron to provide base cover and ground-support, to land on Momote and Manus in February and March 1944. The Kittyhawks' squadrons had assisted in the landings on New Britain at the end of 1943. In the Admiralty Islands, 77 Squadron experimented with the

Above : Liberator rises from Darwin field. *Left :* Beaufighter takes off in New Guinea

use of belly tanks as incendiary weapons. After the tanks had been been filled with captured Japanese fuel, the armourers wired an American incendiary grenade to each tank, the grenade setting off the fuel as the tank hit the ground. Japanese machine gun nests were well protected – being dug-outs with earth-covered palm logs over them and normally US ground forces had to resort to flame-throwers to kill the enemy within. It was hoped that the 'belly-tank bomb' would save the soldiers from the risky necessity of getting close enough to use flame-throwers. Sometimes such targets, and other Japanese fortified positions, were successfully hit and burned out.

RAAF Kittyhawk squadrons provided the bulk of fighter cover during the Allied advances towards the Celebes. Another five squadrons which had been formed on the mainland were now on operations. On 27th July, sixteen Kittyhawks from 86 Squadron, based at Merauke in Dutch New Guinea, climbed too slowly to intercept a small raid, but on 9th September they gained enough altitude to shoot down two Zekes and an Oscar without loss to themselves. Boomerangs also scrambled for this interception, but they were too slow to catch the bombers, let alone the fighters. With sixteen bombers and sixteen fighters in the enemy formations, the Kittyhawk IVs should have claimed more victims although Japanese fighters flew close protective formation with their bombers, flying above, on either side and behind, usually in groups of at least three. The main reason for the comparative lack of success was that thickening oil, the old bugbear, had caused failure in forty-one guns in ten of the P-40s. The RAAF pilots were disappointed since opportunities to engage enemy aircraft were becoming fewer in this area.

Tomahawk pilot has a final word with ground staff before leaving on a mission

In Allied advances, fighter-bombers proved to be the most useful aircraft of all, for a squadron or flight of them could be brought up to a newly-cleared, and often small, newly-captured field and go into action with less facilities than those required by two-engined aircraft. They could not only provide devastating support with a wide assortment of bombs on both hostile troop and coastal shipping targets, but could also be used most effectively for spotting enemy movement and for spraying the jungle with machine gun fire. For the operation at Wakde Island – off the northern coast of Dutch New Guinea – in May, 78 and 80 squadrons were attached to the US 310th Bombardment Group engaged in attacking barges and troops. During a Japanese counterattack at the Tor river, the US ground controller called up the P-40s to make a strike on the advancing Japanese. The army commander later reported to group headquarters: 'Close support mission early this date tremendous success. Air strike broke up Japanese counterattack on our bridgehead across the Tor river.'

78 Squadron eventually found fighter work when fifteen of their aircraft patrolling over Biak were directed to intercept a loose formation of twelve Oscars escorting three Kate torpedo-bombers. The Kittyhawks first climbed into the sun to have it behind them when they attacked in four succeeding sections. A long battle ensued, the Kittyhawks taking turns to join up into groups of seven to act as top cover while the others made their diving passes. In the first pass the leader shot a Kate down in flames into the sea and another pilot shot down two Oscars, the pilot of one being picked up by a US destroyer which had probably been the intended target of the Kates. Then the combat thickened, as the RAAF History records: 'Flight-Lieutenant White, who led Blue section (four Kittyhawks) into the action, which had turned into a furious dogfight of turning, diving,

Right : Kittyhawks armed with 250lb bombs taxi toward take-off point. Ground crew perched on wings direct pilots whose forward view is restricted when their machines are in tail-down attitude. *Below :* Ground crew of No 450 Squadron in Malta prepare Kittyhawks for an operation
Below right : China ; fighters and transports are repaired and serviced by Chinese and American mechanics and technicians

rolling and skidding aircraft, shot two enemy planes down and damaged another. White's fire blasted the wing off another which crashed into the sea. He then chased a Kate which he hit, and the aircraft went into the sea on its back. Altogether, 78 destroyed seven Oscars and two Kates, and damaged one Oscar and one Kate, for the loss of one Kittyhawk and its pilot.'

This was the last time RAAF Kittyhawks were involved in a dogfight mix-up with Japanese fighters in New Guinea. On 10th June 78 Squadron claimed the shooting down of the last Japanese aircraft destroyed in the area. The Kittyhawk's operational use was concentrated on patrols and ground support. Scarcity of enemy fighter opposition meant that they could carry out most of their duties in comparative safety. During May and June a Kittyhawk wing, 78, flew more sorties than any other Allied fighter group: 1,607 in May and 1,454 in June, totalling 8,438 flying hours for the two months.

In October 1944, the squadrons were included in the new formation of First Tactical Air Force, RAAF, and at the end of the year were operating from bases as far as Morotai in the Halmaheras, a group of islands south of the Philippines. Leyte had been invaded by an enormous invasion force which had formed in the Admiralty Islands. All squadrons were by now fitted with bomb racks for army co-operation work bombing in the various areas where the cut-off Japanese troops were still resisting. There were so many Kittyhawks, and other Allied fighters and bombers, and so few targets, that even one barge or a small grass hut received elaborate treatment when it was spotted. Airfields where Japanese aircraft might survive the constant armed reconnaissance were pitted with craters, and any unfortunate Japanese reconnaissance aircraft picked up on one of the numerous radar screens was doomed, no matter how high or low it flew.

Beyond the Celebes is Borneo, an island large enough to accommodate all the land area of the Philippines. Japan was now a target for bombing and was being studied preparatory to a planned invasion so it was unnecessary to invade Borneo. However, it was decided to send in the AIF, and all Kittyhawks to be used in the operation were held on the ground while thorough servicing prepared them for action. Tarakan and Balikpapan were the first objectives on the island which was invaded at the end of April 1945. The landing at Tarakan was unopposed, the enemy having withdrawn inland after a severe bombing by Allied bombers and fighters. The airfield was cleared of mines and snipers after the fifth day so that the army could have closer support. On such a large island the enemy could occasionally bring in an aircraft unnoticed but these were usually discovered and destroyed. A sample of Kittyhawk work during one month's operation is this record of one squadron in July:
'The Japanese Headquarters situated at Sapong was attacked on several occasions. The Keningau-Ranur Road was bombed and strafed, also Pensiangan, Tomani, Tengoa, Tambunan, Takarut in the Ranau area, Beaufort, Beluru and Melalab. Enemy troop concentrations were attacked at Beluru township, the junction of the Nyabor and Bakong rivers, Pensiangan, Lenom area, Beaufort and the Lambir area. Watercraft sweeps were carried out along the Rajong river from Sibu to Song and from Kanowit to Siba. Armed reconnaissance missions were completed from Langkon to Matinggong. Enemy ammunition dumps and dispersal areas were attacked on every occasion and the enemy's Trusan River bases were devastated in co-operation with army units.'

The 2nd November raid which devastated Rabaul harbour. Both shipping and shore installations blaze in the general destruction

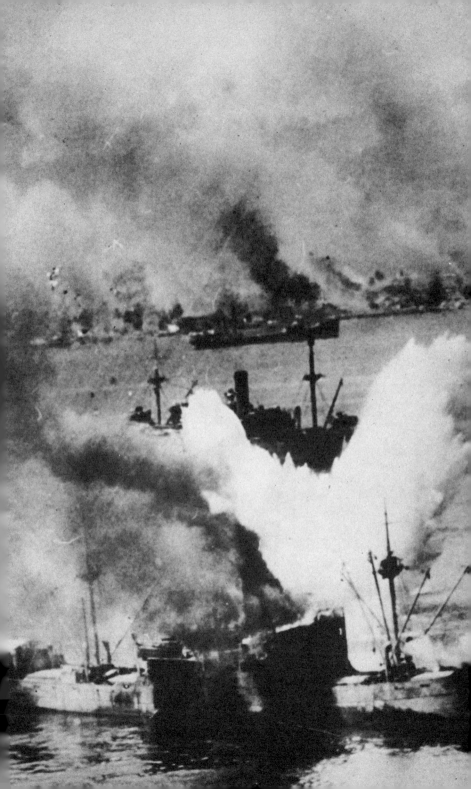

Left : Chinese soldier stands guard as US ground crew service a P-40
Above : A well-loaded Kitty-bomber is guided to take off-point

Above : Captured 'Hamp' at Buna, New
Guinea, airstrip
Above right : Smashed Japanese planes
at Lae
Right : Towards the end of the fighting
in China. Captured Zero with Chinese
markings ; Warhawk in background

Two seater conversion from
P-40N-5 with drop tank

Two seater conversions from P-40N-30...

...and from P-40N-35

Tomahawk IIB pictured from its most favourable angle

**Near Ledo Road, Upper Burma;
US Warhawks swoop in to land after
mission is accomplished**

And from 76 Squadron records: 'On 27th May, thirteen aircraft in conjunction with the 13th Air Force and PT boats carried out what amounted to a "blitz" on the North Borneo town of Sandakan. Great destruction was caused and it created so much excitement among the Nipponese that Tokyo Radio announced a landing and the enemy troops hastily retreated to the interior.'

The Kittyhawks were still operating at Borneo, where only a few pockets of isolated enemy resistance survived in the hills, when the war ended.

In December 1944, P-40 production had ceased. The last of over 14,000 built was a P-40N-40-CU which looked much the same as the original P-40D except for cutaway decking behind the cockpit. Before production ended Curtiss had made a bid to catch the

attention of Allied air forces with the XP-40Q interceptor. In 1943 a P-40K had been modified with the 'beard' radiators discarded and replaced by radiators in the wings so that the slimmed, pointed nose gave less drag. In another experiment a bubble canopy had been fitted to a P-40L and an N, both of which had cut down rear fuselages. With a basic P-40K airframe and a 1,425 hp water-injection Allison V-1710-121 engine driving a four-blade constant-speed airscrew, the XP-40Q featured the experimental radiators fitted into the wings near the roots, and the bubble canopy over the slimmed fuselage. With clipped wings the XP-40Q-2 was capable of a maximum speed of 422mph.

Other Curtiss experimental fighters also possessed potentially high speed performances for operations: the XP-55 Ascender, an Allison-engined pusher type with elevators positioned at the nose, the rudders at the wing-

tips, and with a tricycle undercarriage, had a maximum speed of 390mph; the experimental P-60s, which were fitted with either in-line Allisons or Pratt & Whitney radials to fly at 420 mph; and the XP-62, powered by a Wright-Cyclone eighteen-cylinder radial engine, was expected to fly at 448mph and be armed with four 20mm cannon. But there were better fighter and fighter-bomber aircraft coming off other assembly rigs in 1944 and the historic line of Curtiss wartime fighters ended with the P-40N.

The P-40 victories in the Second World War were established by courageous pilots who dogfought and dive-bombed under the worst conditions that could be experienced in the sub-Arctic, deserts and tropics. The battles were won by its pilots whose varied qualities of airmanship won out against an initially better-equipped foe; the machine itself was an indifferent design stamped out in almost continuous repetition of the original Curtiss formula, yet it was flown to more victories than defeats against superior aircraft. Its transformation to bomb-carrying gave the Allies an unexpected extra weapon that proved to be invaluable for close ground-support. P-40 fame is recorded in the annals of all Allied air force histories, and in the songs composed by pilots who flew it into action, songs of squadrons and planes, and sad and comical songs, too joyfully coarse to be recorded, of their comrades, incidents and fatalities –

'Beside his shattered Kittyhawk
The young "peelo" he lay,
Come listen to the very last words
The young "peelo" did say:
'I'm going to a better land
Where everything is bright,
Where whisky grows on the coconut trees
And they play poker every night...'

This history is also a memorial to those 'peelos' who lost their lives in Curtiss P-40s.

XP-40Q, almost the final version of the
hard-worked P-40, never flew in action

Bibliography

The AAF in Australia USAAF Historical Division (US Air University, Maxwell, Alabama)
Air Action in the Papuan Campaign USAAF Historical Division (US Air University, Maxwell, Alabama)
World War II in the Air Major James F Sunderman (Franklin Watts, New York)
Fighter Aces T Constable and R Tolliver (Barker, London)
The Army Air Forces in World War II (7 volumes) Ed W L Craven and J L Cate (Chicago)
Retreat from Kokoda Raymond Paull (Panther, London)
MacArthur 1941-1951: Victory in the Pacific Major-Generals Charles A Willoughby and John Chamberlain (Heinemann, London)
New Zealand in the Air War Alan W Mitchell (Harrap, London)
USAAF Fighters 1916-1961 Bruce Robertson (Harleyford, Letchworth, England)
God is My Co-pilot Colonel Robert L Scott (Ballantine, New York. Hodder & Stoughton, London)
War-planes of Yesteryear Kenneth G Munson (Arco, New York. Ian Allen, Walton-on-Thames)